MY AFRICAN

BLACK BOOK

BY

VINCENT HAPPY MNISI

Contents

Introduction

This book is written to enlighten the Black Races of the world. Its main aim is to awaken the African Spirit of African Spiritualism and to encourage African Socialism to replace Capitalism worldwide. For this book to have any relevance today and the current state of Africa, I must do a Historical study of the European Race to try to understand their nature off subjection and their self-entitlement to rule over and control the wealth of the World. All research for this book has been internet based, my research and all the information in this book is available for those that are interested to know who controls the world we live in. I have also done a historical study of the foundations of Christianity and a Historical study of the European Dark years of Witchcraft and Paganism.

I have also done a historical study of the birth of The Roman Catholic Church and its connections with paganism rituals and Ethiopian Orthodox Church. I have also done a historical study of the Wars the Roman Catholic Churches fought in Europe and the World. This book had to try and understand European Enlightenment and this study is also to try and over stand their idealism of them wanting to conquer the World for their Crowns. This book tries to understand the need for European miseducation and the need to instil a superiority complex in their populations and the world through their education and religious systems which have had such a negative effect on the black looking masses who have become mentally enslaved by their systems. I also did a historical research study on secret societies i.e. Freemason; Club of Rome; Skull & Bones; the elusive Illuminati and their involvement in world affairs and the Vatican. I then did a historical study of the origins of current and past Social Economic Systems E.g. Capitalism; Communism; European Socialism V African Socialism.

This book has taken a historical and current state of the African Royal Heritage. This book investigates the origins of Slavery; Colonialism; Imperialism; Neo-Imperialism and Colonialism not forgetting African fake Independence. This book aims to enlighten and awaken African Spiritualism. This book highlights the activism of Pan-Africanism from 1800 to date. Africa needs to be united structurally on the Economic; Political, Social as decided in the recent African Union meeting in Kigali Rwanda in March 2018. Africa needs a social service system that will benefit African people and not the European populations. Africa needs a Pan-Africanism that will work for the African people and by ensuring a stable African Society.

Africa needs to start now setting millennium goals, fifty-year goals and twenty years goals of educating our youth to be able to communicate with the world and to communicate within itself by educating our youth a Universal African Language.

I began writing this book on Easter Sunday 1^{St} of April 2018 April Fool's day because it has a huge significance to the state of the world we live in today. This current state the world is nothing, but an illusion and the sooner Africans wake up the sooner the tables will be turned from Europe being a First World Continent and Africa being graded as a Third World Continent. The Current Capitalistic; Imperialistic state of current affairs the world finds itself in is due to a couple of factors and systems of which I am going to try and break them down as simply as I can. For this to make sense to the reader I will start with a brief biography of myself and why I feel compelled to write and enlighten people willing to read.

I was born on Easter Sunday at 6.05 a.m. on the 29th of March 1970 in my Grandfathers house in Soweto South Africa. Been born into Apartheid South Africa I was forced to leave aged six years old after the 1976 Soweto Student Uprising. I was shipped to a Roman Catholic Boarding School in my Mum's native country Rhodesia now Zimbabwe. I attended the Sacred Heart Bushsticks Roman Catholic Boarding School during the intense guerrilla warfare being waged by the Zipra and Zanla forces against the Ian Smith UDI regime. The school was protected by the Rhodesian Army who had a fort nearby. As an impressionable child aged six and now living and being schooled by White people and attending their Church which had a white Jesus and Saints and even a White Mary too. I believe that is then, when I became brainwashed into believing that white people were more superior than black people because they were made in Jesus's image and the saint's too.

I have been doing a lot of soul searching of late during my research for this book which has changed my whole perspective of the way I view life and the world as we know it and my viewpoints have changed tremendously in such a way and I hope it does the same for you after reading this book. Sunday 1st April 2018 April Fool's Day lol. The world has been fed a big Con-Story by a cabal of European families that have set up systems to ensure that they stay in control of the World's resources and its population too.

Religious Systems

The Ethiopian Orthodox Church is the largest African Orthodox Christian Church. It is one of the few pre-colonial Christian Churches in Sub-Saharan Africa. The Ethiopian Orthodox Tewahedo Chucrh has a membership of between 45 and 50 million followers the majority of whom live in Ethiopia. The Ethiopian Orthodox Tawahedo Chucrh is in communion with the Coptic Orthodox Church of Alexandria having gained autocephaly in 1959. It had been administratively part of the Coptic Orthodox Church of Alexandria from the first half of the 4th Century until 1959 when it was granted its own Patriarch by the Coptic Orhodox Pope of Alexandra. I have noticed that their depiction of the image of Mary and Christ are of Black African Jewish origin even to this day.

Tawahedo mean's "Being made one" referring to the Orthodox belief in being perfectly unified in the nature of Christ. i.e. a complete union of the divine and Human Natures into one nature is self-evident inorder to accomplish the divine salvation of humankind as opposed to the two nature of Christ belief commonly held by the Roman catholic; Anglican, Lutheran and most other Protestant Church. Miaphysitism holds that in the one person of Jesus Christ, Divinity and Humanity are united in one nature without separation without confusion without alteration and without mixing where Christ is consubstantial with God the Father is as much as he is with mankind. Around 500 Bishops within the Patriarchates of Alexandria; Antioch and Jerusalem refused to accept the Dyophysitism doctrine decreed by the Council of Chalcedon in 451 and incident that resulted in the first major split in the main body of the Christian faith.

The period of the Jesuit's influence which broke the connection with Egypt began a new chapter in the Roman Catholic Church history. The Roman Empire officially adopted Christianity in AD 380. During the Early Middle ages most of Europe underwent Christianisation. Many attribute Christianity for being the link that created a unified European Identity. With the rise from Islam from the 8th Century a constellation that led to the Catholic Crusade Wars which were unsuccessful militarily but where an important step in the emergence of a united religious identity in Europe. The Great Schism of the 11th century and reformation of the 16th century was a tear apart Christendom into hostile factions we see today following the Age of Enlightenment of the 18th century, Atheism and Agnosticism has spread across Europe.

Paganism is a term first used in the fourth century by early Christians for the people who practiced Polytheism either because they were increasingly rural and didn't know Christ. Christianity emerged from the second Temple of Judaism developing as one of the several monotheistic cults during the 18th Century. The European Race is a very strange race indeed with their histories of interclan clashes and so-called World War's. Their biggest con story began in Constantie's Times when Christianity was founded by simulating several schools of beliefs into one religion. I did a historical study of the Ethiopian Church and my finding astonished me and couldn't help but notice the similarities with the Roman Catholic Church.

The Ethiopian Church believe in Yeshua who was also born on 25th December to a virgin Mother who went on to do the same things that their claim their White Blue Eyes Jesus went on to do. My study of the Ethiopian Church Doctrine exposes the Roman Catholic Church of stealing their beliefs systems and placing the Handsome gay nephew of an ex-Pope's to pose as Jesus Christ. The Roman Catholic was established for false missionary purposes and to amass as much wealth and property as they could get their hands on. All churches today are very wealth creation driven with their constant rhetoric of tithing giving 10% of your earnings to your church has been drummed into congregation's time and time again before passing the collection baskets. I question tithing and what is has led Christians into believing that their need to pay their pastors 10% of their earnings in order to receive blessing from God is totally ridicules and outrages. Have you ever asked yourself what makes these Pastors Multi-Millionaires affording to travel via private jets? The Roman Catholic's were famous for selling Heaven tickets to its elderly congregation a practise still been practised today with the church gaining from their estates after their pass on.

The Confession room's in the Catholic Church System makes one wonder what kind of power their fathers claim to have the power to absolve sin. I don't believe that any human being has that power not matter how holy they have been all their lives apart from God and no Catholic Priest has that power on Earth to absolve my sins on Earth. These confession room's in the Catholic System gives you insight on the kind of power the church wanted to attain from their congregations by knowing all their secrets is astonishing and to think that we still have confessions to this very day. I have concluded and come to an understanding that there is only one God that can absolve my sin's.

Capitalism is another system built to ensure that large Corporations whose foundations can be traced back to Slavery, Colonisation, Imperialism and Neo-Imperialism will continue to own the worlds wealth which are in the hands and controlled by European run companies and establishments. The current world's biggest corporations; NGO and Governments have been predominately led by Europeans who have closes tie to one or more of the Secretive Societies. These Secretive Societies John F Kennedy spoke about in his speech in 1964 appoint Company Directors; Managing Directors of Multinational Companies, NGO's and even select who is going to run for Prime Ministership and Presidency in all countries with a Rothchild Reserve Bank.

This Capitalistic world we live in now is full off cheats, scoundrels, manipulative individuals and companies wanting in on the next big idea. They swamp on any latest innovation like bees do to honey. They break down products and recreate their own brands in order to create competition which is at times very unwarranted behaviour and causes losses for the innovators. Capitalism is just pure evil thievery cunning European mentally which is to discover lands that people live in and claim to invent products/services that were already invented by other Races. I will just but list just a few inventions that were claimed by Europeans when they were invented by African Americans and Indians too. One question I have for the pro-capitalist system is "Companies are undying entities if they remain profitable right? Why create something that will outlive you amassing Hugh profits and not giving back to the community that is keeping them profitable?

I propose that all companies should issue 20% shares to workers in their annual profits. My argument is that workers contribute as much as the owner to make sure that the company remains profitable and hence should be rewarded profitably accordingly. Work is economic slavery in disguise and now everybody in the world is out to get themselves as much worthless paper they can get hold off that we call money. They get paid in a bank account and that money is then used by the bankers to make more money from their money they must deposited into their banks, this world is a Bankers Paradise and they are the only ones profiting from everybody that is living today.

Inflation is another made up fallacy my recent visit to South Africa was shocking for me to find that their priced their bread at R10, come on? The price of growing wheat never changes right? and they are paying low wages then what is the excuse of making such a price, The Financial Auditors need to check their books because it seems like there are making 1000% profits from a subsistence product which should be made as cheap as possible. The problem is that all companies in South Africa are pegging their prices with the Pound and what you buy for 1 pound in England it's worth R10 in South Africa which is fraud the financial regulators are sleeping in South Africa.

Going back to my upbringing, I flew for the first time on my own aged 8 years old to visit my family in Soweto from Bulawayo Airport in Zimbabwe to then Jan-Smuts Airport in 1978, I recall that I was terrified but thanks to the friendly Airhostess who looked after me throughout the terrifying journey. After the school holidays my Mother decided to take my younger twin brothers along with, Siphwe who has passed on now R.I.P my dear brother who suffered from birth effect complications needed medical certification before crossing the border and we had to disembark from the train at 12pm with nowhere to sleep luckily one of the African police officers offered us his concrete living room floor.

What happened next will always stay on my mind for eternity because what I was about to witness made me believe that there was a God and that he was watching over me and my family. Our next train was delayed due to the fact that our previous compartment was bazooked the night before. I couldn't believe my eyes when our next train passed our previous coach on its side with a big hole in the compartment we were previously in the night before. I just wanted to give you a glimpse of how my life has been blessed by God from an early age the is more still come so just keep reading. I have always believed in my Ancestors even with my Christian upbringing, I have always maintained my beliefs that my Ancestors were in heaven with God and were always fighting for my corner always because I have been blessed with opportunities a prince would wish for. In 1979 during the transition government of Bishop Abel Muzorewa and Ian Smith my Mum arranged for me to travel ahead from Bulawayo to Harare and get dropped off at the ZRBC stations in Harare/Salisbury where I was to meet up with Mandisa Mundwarara who then took me to her Father's house in Borrowdale. I just recall that it had some many bedrooms and I was given one double bedroom to use while I awaited my mother.

In 1980 my mum enrolled us into David Livingstone primary School in Harare. My highlight at the Independence celebration was the fact that I got to dance with Bob Marley during his Exodus song, I am the kid in the brown and that I also that got to meet Joshua Nkomo too aged 10.

Aged 11 my Mum shipped me to Boarding school again this time to Godfrey Huggins Primary in Marondera. Where I developed a close friendship with some white kid in my first term, I was shocked when schools started again he didn't want anything to do with me my first lesson in racial prejudices which must have come from the parents because I kinder knew that his parents must have had a word with him hence he started hanging out with his kind only from then onwards. In 1981 Godfrey Huggins Primary must have had only about 10 Black African students in the whole school. Primary boarding life was bliss and I developed the art of dreaming and creating my own little worlds that I lived in as a grown up. I still attended the Roman Catholic Church every Sunday and went through their rituals of reciting prayers in-order for me to start receiving holy communion. I was again in an English establishment being taught by white teachers, having white house matrons I couldn't help but to start to envy the White Race and wondered why I was born Black? All my close friends were white, and we really got along competitively of course. I recall that I had invited my Mother to several swimming gala's that she never did attend but there was one that she did attend and because of that I managed to beat the best swimmer in the school in the Individual medley beating him by a touch.

I was 15 years old when I started High School in 1985 at a School I got to choose myself because an old friend Dumisani Gutu who sadly passed on now rest in peace my dear friend. I was in for a shock treatment of bullying that I had to endure for the three whole years off me attending Allan Wilson High School which was in the City Centre where my Mother lived, and she was not having me becoming a day scholar so I was enrolled into Burnham House which was under the watchful eyes of Clive Barnes who had a mean left hand. I recall running away from been bullied one day and just walked home to complain hoping my Mother would stand up for me, but hay was I wrong because all she did was call for Mr Barnes who came to collect me from my Mum's flat in Union Avenue and gave me six of the best for leaving the school's premises without permission I think I must have received about 200 lashings from Mr Barnes in my three years under his care.

I excelled in sports playing Rugby; Tennis; Gymnastics; Cross Country running; Water Polo; Swimming; Cricket and Hockey. I made the school teams every year too. During some school holidays my brothers would be sent to be with our Grandfather who would travel from Johannesburg to spend the holidays with us at his house which we helped him buy in Khumalo Suburb in Bulawayo.

I got to meet Joshua Nkomo again this time while we watched him get out of a bullet ridden Mercedes Benz which was bullet proof he shocked me by coming across to me and asking me how my mother was, I was very amazed because I didn't recall meeting him and told him that she was fine and he told me to tell her that he wants to see her and that I should convey the message to her, I had forgotten that we had met in 1980 and after I told my mother she was also shocked that he could recall me after five years. I heard from people that Joshua Nkomo had a photographic memory.

In 1987 my mum enrolled me into Churchill Boys High School into another boarding house called Spencer House with my younger brother Sipho to keep an eye on him and keep him from being bullied as she knew that I was being bullied but never did nothing about it. In 1987 the Graceland Concert organised by Paul Simon came into town where I got to meet Hugh Masekela; Ray Phiri and Miriam Makeba may their souls rest in peace too. Miss Chaka Chaka even came to our Boarding House and played the piano for the boys and the teachers who began to look at us with different eyes from then onwards.

To top it off during one of my school holidays I meet up with loads of South African's who were in exile too and was advised by Themba Ndaba to apply for Scholarships after I had told him that my mother pays our school fees and all he wanted to know was can I get hold of our South African Birth Certificates and I told yes and from then I went and stole them from my Mum's hiding place and he took me to an Office at the University of Zimbabwe World University Services of Canada operated from there and once I had registered my brothers and I we began getting our school fees paid for and they gave us each a Zim$ 1000 monthly which helped my mother tremendously as they continued to pay our school fees for a further five years until 1991.

I took a keen interest in the politics in Zimbabwe and always listened to Robert Mugabe's eloquent speech's and would often consult the dictionary every time he spoke, I have to thank him for he did improve my English drastically as I was growing up learning about the South African Struggle against the Apartheid Regime in South Africa at the time when I met some ANC; Black Consciousness Movement and P.A.C South African exiles too. I can recall telling myself then aged 18 that I would one day meet up with Nelson Mandela.

In 1991 the year that he was released from prison, I was 21 years old then and hungry for life and had just completed a London Chamber of Commerce and Industry LCCI diploma in Marketing, Public Relations and Commerce at CCOSA College in Harare Zimbabwe. We as a family repatriated back to South Africa under the United Nation's Repatriation Scheme which saw us been reunited with my Mother family in Soweto for a while. With the help from the ANC I enrolled into the Associations of Advertising Agencies School of Advertising in Rosebank Johannesburg and later moved to Cape Town so that I could get the housing element of the scholarship fund.

In 1994 I voted for the ANC and Mandela, I then arranged for a letter from the ANC to Hunt Lascaris TBWA the Advertising agency that was handling the ANC Advertising Account to employ me. I eventually lived through my daydream in 1995 of meeting Nelson Mandela when as I was about shake his hand he shocked me by saying "So you are Vincent Mnisi" and I was amazed that he knew my name and I just replied "Yes Sir" and then he went on to say "You are doing a good job for us" and I just stated "Thank you sir" I also got to meet up with Jacob Zuma and Cyril Ramaphosa too.

In 1997 my ex-wife got pregnant with my only child and since she was from Cape Town she felt that she should be closer to her family when she gave birth. I left Hunt Lascaris TBWA Johannesburg and joined Young & Rubicam Cape Town handling their Gilbeys Liquor brands and Good Year Tyres. I got headhunted by AWSG JWT Cape Town and I joined them on the Nike Account which I handled from 1997 to 1999 when I left them because of their child labour scandal in China. I moved on and joined P4 Radio as their Strategic planner for their airtime Sales team.

I was then asked by an American Investor to help him set up a business helping African get loans and set up business in Cape Town. I arranged for my first client who happened to be my Mother a bank loan to start a Hair Salon, I was blind to see that this was my meal ticket and I had a fall out with the investor which led to my marriage break up as I was suddenly unemployed, and my ex-wife had to get a Job for the first time. I moved back to Johannesburg after she got me locked up after a fight during Christmas of 1999 and New Year's, she only came to bail me out on the 3rd of January 2000. That was the last time I saw her as I left for Johannesburg soon after my release from Palls Mall Prison.

I joined MTN as their Marketing Assistant to the Marketing Manager I was there for only two months when I was headhunted by 8 Seconds Advertising to handle their MTN advertising business. Sadly, I was only there for three months only because I had a mental breakdown because of my marriage break-up they paid me off with R120 000 disability grant and told me that if I did improve I could come back. I left for Bulawayo where my Mother and daughter had relocated back too as she had inherited my Grand Fathers House after he got shot 11 bullets in a Taxi Warfare in Johannesburg.

I recuperated in Bulawayo Zimbabwe for two years spending some quality time with my Mother, Brother and daughter too who had lived with my mother from a very early age while my ex-wife attended College. We then decided as a family to travel to the UK, my brother and I first travelled together and then my Mother and daughter followed us three years later. When we went to apply for our Zimbabwean Passports we went via John Nkomo's Zimbabwe Home Office Minister at that time who made sure that we got our passports within a week of application. The UK was another rude awakening too where I realised that there was also a class system in place within Europeans and that they have semi-cultural differences according to provinces and countries too. I have now lived worked and studied in the UK for the past 15 years writing five books and attaining two BA Hon's degrees in Advertising and Brand Management and Business Management and an MSc in Marketing Communications.

One thing that I found out when I moved to the United Kingdom is how deep-rooted racism; bigotry and pure ignorance was in their societies, I began to question their education and upbringing. The racist remarks I would get from strangers made me wonder and once my neighbours five-year-old began singing Baba Black sheep every time he saw me. I went and told my housing officer and they went and told the police, imagine that Police Officers had to come and tell this child aged 6 years old that he was being racist by singing that song every time he saw me. I don't blame the kid as I think or assume that his parents must have been calling me Baba Black Sheep and he was just coping them. I also got some trouble from the white teenagers who used to throw rocks and rotten apples at my house I had to call the police about a dozen times in the three years I lived there.

Europeans have pulled the biggest trick in the world by firstly stealing our doctrines of Christianity and Judaism and turning it into their doctrines as it has been discovered lately that some African tribes have the original Jewish genetic blood cells of the original Jews from Israel. Europeans have been stealing inventions created by other races and making them their own. Like the Akerzarin European Jews that are currently occupying Palestine have no connection with the Israel apart from them adopting Judaism as religion while still in Eastern Europe and have not rightful claim over Israel. This book will prove that Hitler knew of their evil plans and was aware that the Original Jews were African's and I have read some his translated speeches where he states that.

The European's capitalism system has allowed them to steal and innovate other people's ideas and religious doctrines all in the name of Capitalism. The backbone of Capitalism in its current form was built by the theft of African Slaves; Colonialism; Imperialism; Neo-Imperialism and now Fake Independences granted to African countries while the Europeans have full control of the economies of every African state even printing their monies for the Ex-French Colonies and still in charge of all the other Reserve banks of the world too. The Rothchild have a stack in every currency that is being printed in Africa and can make or break it in the World markets as they control the London Stock exchange where currencies values are decided. Before granting Independence in each African Country their resources were purposely sold off to private entities with there UN; IMF and the World Bank offering crippling loans against their resources no wonder countries like Zimbabwe and Zambia were crippled when they had arguments with their Reserves bank owners.

Hence, they began printing ridiculous notes such a 1 million Zimbabwe Dollar notes and the Zambian 1 million Kwacha too. Their currencies were taken to the mud when Kaunda and Mugabe tried to get rid of the Rothchild's from owning their Reserve bank. The rights to Africa's mineral wealth is now in the hands of European, American and Chinese investors whom are making a killing from exploiting African rich mineral deposit. One sad fact and example is Zambia selling of their Copper deposit to a private Company who have made a killing from it and have not yet paid their appropriate taxes that they are supposed to pay to them and their extraction methods have also caused sickness to the community living close to the mine too.

European; American and Chinese economies are now heavily depended on their exploitative mineral rights that they have in Africa through their Multinational companies which are controlled by the Freemason's; Skull and Bones and Illuminati graduates. Graduates from these Secretive Societies are appointed to political; business and religious positions of power and I shall go into more detail later in the book. Coming back to my mini biography which I hope will lead you to understand how I came about my understandings I am about to reveal to you in this book. I began to write "Africa Must Unite" in 2010, soon followed by "The United Countries of Africa Now" in 2011 and then I put together a Book of my favourite quotes and my own quotes too into a book I called Inspire Aspire for Assertiveness in 2013; I then wrote my first Fictional storyline I called the Adventures of an African Dealer. I then I wrote Life! Which is a Black Christian motivational book as my fifth book and this one is going to be my sixth one. Whenever I write I feel this breath of fresh air blow over my head and at times used to irritate me because it would be there for days on end. My mother told me that it was the Glory of the Holy Spirit blessing my work.

I have had two prophesies on my life by well know Prophets such as Cindy Jacobs and Kirk Bennett who have both told me that they see me speaking and been listened too by hundreds of thousands of people at once. I am now hoping to make that prophecy a reality by my declaring now that I intend to enter Politics and I am currently engaged with talks with a WhatsApp group of Pan Africanist. My Pro- Pan-Africanist propaganda that I have been posting on Facebook has really got my name out there and I have received over 120 000 likes in three months not mentioning the number of shares too. I was getting likes every second at some stage Facebook decided to ban me from posting on to pages that I am not in control off.

My narrative from the beginning when I began writing my books was to enlighten the African Race and drive for a United Africa politically; economically and culturally. A united Africa which does not look to the West or East for idea's and financial backing but looks within itself to generate the next biggest Ideas and capital too.

When Europeans in 1881 in Germany divided and carved up Africa like a cake between themselves and took it themselves to miseducated us of our true heritage on earth we have now become the 3rd world nations always begging for American and European Inked paper money with no real added value apart from stolen gold that sit's in their reserve banks because I am quite sure that they are no gold mines in England. They give us worthless inked paper in exchange for our minerals. Africa Must Wake up it's time, South Africa has taken the lead by stating that they were getting all the Mineral and land Rights back into Governments hands and leasing it out that is a beginning. After much research and soul searching I have realised that Europeans are a sick race and need to payback the world for they evil ways of Slavery and Colonisation. They are still practising Neo-Imperialism games with Africa to this day.

Quite relevant to all this, I have made several points above. One was that, notwithstanding the European well-developed systems of maintaining disunity within the African race, he is still disturbed by any signs of a movement towards unity among Africans and goes into action in many subtle ways to offset it. The important point is the most disheartening. But as in the history of Africa, not one of these, standing alone, can meet the mounting crisis of the African race If we don't unite. Africa needs a people's mass organization movement which will override all these systems and pull the thoughts and needs of the African Race and fulfil its destiny in life without any help from Eastern or European systems.

African's are in themselves indications of weakness, because they becloud their own mind with European Propaganda which prevents them from calm and clear thinking that is absolutely required for planning if the African Race is to be saved from final destruction by the European Race. The only hope for the kind of racial unity that will really liberate Africans to command the respect of the world will be to unite politically, economically, socially and culturally like it's never before attempted.

This will require a new kind of leadership, a leadership with the single purpose of helping African to start building a better life for themselves without the influence from Europe, China and the USA. This is inevitable in our circumstances of our currencies in the hands of Europeans. But as in the history of Africa, not one of these, standing alone, can meet the mounting crisis of the Economic race the world is in now using African resources. If Africa does not unite, the African race will parish into worse poverty than it is now.

Jesuits Order and Secret Societies

The Jesuit Order was created by Catholic Ignatius Loyola in 1500s to counter the Reformation and uplift the authority of the Papacy. They principles are based on this statement he made "Finally, let all with such artfulness gain the ascendant over princes, noblemen, and the magistrates of every place, that they may be ready at our beck, even to sacrifice their nearest relations and most intimate friends, when we say it is for our interest and advantage"

The world's wars and all wars in Europe in the earlier years and all revolutions occur because the Jesuits made them happen with their ultimate ambition to establish a one-world government with the Papacy at its head. Even over a century ago their plans were to take over Countries and each time succeeding, as 19th-century theologian Luigi De Sanctis tells us "At what then do the Jesuits aim? According to them, they only seek the greater glory of God; but if you examine the facts you will find that they aim at universal dominion alone. They have rendered themselves indispensable to the Pope, who, without them, could not exist, because Catholicism is identified with them. They have rendered themselves indispensable to governors and hold revolutions in their hands; and in this way, either under one name or another, it is they who rule the world" As the sources below attest, the Jesuits have been involved in and even spearheaded many of the world's worst wars, revolutions, and massacres.

At times, the Jesuits are directly involved, at other times, they use their influence over the Freemasons and other secret societies. The Jesuits and other Secret Societies have links to Catholicism and their aims of being very powerful. There might be hints, but few see the fullness. This is because the Papacy doesn't want people to know how much political clout it holds. To prevent opposition, the Papacy uses the Jesuits to build its political empire. The Jesuits have been active in forming other holy orders, such as the Knights of Peter Claver and the Knights of Columbus, over which they retain immense control. For it is an old trick on the part of the sons of Loyola, that whenever their Order is under threat or suspicion they swell their numbers by means of the sodalities of creating 'new' orders. Moreover, the Pope has thousands of secret agents worldwide. They include Jesuits, the Knights of Columbus, Knights of Malta, Opus Dei, and others.

The Vatican's Intelligence Service and its field resources are second to none. There is considerable analogy between Masonic and Jesuitic degrees; and the Jesuits also tread down the shoe and bare the knee, because Ignatius Loyola thus presented himself at Rome and asked for the confirmation of his order from the Pope. The religion of Freemasonry is essentially the worship of Lucifer, or Satan. In Masonic thought, Satan is the light-bearer, and God is the dark one. This is typical Gnostic inversion of the truth one of Satan's favorite deceptions.

"Humanism" a Religion of self the idea that "man is a god in the making" is another of Satan's lies taught in Masonry, as these Masonic sources states, Masonry teaches that redemption and salvation are both the power and the responsibility of the individual Mason. Every man in essence is his own savior and Redeemer; for if he does not save himself, he will not be saved our goal is to create harmony within the lodge and to improve ourselves, spiritually, intellectually, morally; in all aspects of our lives. The perfect man is Christ: and Christ is God. This is the birth-right and destiny of every human soul...It is far more important that men should strive to become Christs than that they should believe that Jesus was Christ. Be still and know that I am God... 'that I am God,' the final recognition of the All in All, the unity of the Self with the Cosmos the cognition of the divinity of the self."

"Ecumenism" is this divinity of self-appeals to people of many religions. Freemasonry allows use of any scripture, and worship at any altar perpetuating the universal religion that satisfies them all. "We permit Jewish and Muslim brethren to content themselves with the books of the Old Testament or Koran. Masonry does not interfere with the peculiar form or development of any one's religious faith. All that it asks is that the interpretation of the symbol shall be in accordance to what each one supposes to be the revealed will of the creator. The true Mason is not creed-bound. He realizes with the divine illumination of his lodge that as a Mason his religion must be universal Christ, Buddha or Mohammed, the name means little, for he recognizes only the light and not the bearer. He worships at every shrine, bows before every altar, whether in temple. mosque or cathedral, realizing with his truer understanding the oneness of all spiritual truth."

The Bible is an indispensable part of the furniture of a Christian Lodge, only because it is the sacred book of the Christian religion. The Hebrew Pentateuch in a Hebrew Lodge, and the Koran in a Mohammedan one, belong on the Altar; and one of these, and the Square and Compass, properly understood, are the Great Lights by which a Mason must walk and work.

Freemasonry is helping in the Papacy's and New Age movement's mission of joining all the world's religions together, as we are seeing happen in the United Nations, the World Council of Churches, and the ecumenical movement. Learn more about spirituality and secret societies. These stained-glass pictures in the largest Masonic Lodge in Guthrie, Oklahoma are a special feature of this particular lodge. During the day, the figures apparently representing Biblical or famous characters, appear white-skinned. But at night, the figures become dark-skinned. These stained class pieces of art were specially created to achieve this effect in order to signify the white/black their deception out in the open. They are links to the Roman Catholic religion political system that has reigned in varying degrees of power for nearly two millennia. Under the influence of its successive popes, bishops, and cardinals, this system has established an increasing number of doctrines and statements that clearly go against Scripture.

Planning the Three World Wars, in a letter dated January 22, 1870, Italian revolutionary and Illuminati leader Guiseppe Mazzini wrote this to Albert Pike the founder of the KKK in America a 33-degree Freemason.

"We must allow all of the federations to continue just as they are, with their systems, their central authorities and diverse modes of correspondence between high grades of the same rite, organized as they are at present, but we must create a super rite, which will remain unknown, to which we will call those Masons of high degree whom we shall select. With regard to our brothers in Masonry, these men must be pledged to the strictest secrecy. Through this supreme rite, we will govern all Freemasonry which will become the one International Center, the more powerful because its direction will be unknown".

Albert Pike wrote a letter to Mazzini on August 15, 1871, in which he outlined plans for three world wars that were seen as necessary to bring about the One World Order. For a short time, this letter was on display in the British Museum Library in London and it was copied by William Guy Carr, former Intelligence Officer in the Royal Canadian Navy.

"We shall unleash the nihilist and the atheists, and we shall provoke a formidable social cataclysm which in its horror will show clearly to the nations the effect of absolute atheism, origin of savagery and the bloodiest turmoil. Then everywhere, the citizens, obliged to defend themselves against the minority of revolutionaries, will exterminate those destroyers of civilization, and the multitude, disillusioned with Christianity...will receive the pure light through the universal manifestation of the pure doctrine of Lucifer...the destruction of Christianity and atheism. Both conquered and exterminated at the same time. According to threeworldwars.com, these were the purposes of the three world wars Pike and Mazzini had in mind

The First World War: To overthrow the power of the Czars in Orthodox Russia and bring about an atheistic communist state. The Second World War: To originate between Great Britain and Germany. To strengthen communism as antithesis to Judeo-Christian culture and bring about a Zionist State in Israel. The Third World War: A Middle Eastern War involving Judaism and Islam and spreading internationally. Mazzini, with Pike, developed a plan for three world wars so that eventually every nation would be willing to surrender its national sovereignty to a world government. The first war was to end the czarist regime in Russia, and the second war was to allow the Soviet Union to control Europe. The third world war was to be in the Middle East between Moslems and Jews and would result in The Armageddon.

Objective researchers contend that Iran is not being demonized because they are a nuclear threat, just as the Taliban, Iraq's Saddam Hussein and Libya's Muammar Qadaffi were not a threat. What then is the real reason? Is it the trillions to be made in oil profits, or the trillions in war profits? Is it to bankrupt the U.S. economy, or is it to start World War III? Is it to destroy Israel's enemies, or to destroy the Iranian central bank so that no one is left to defy Rothschild's money racket?

Rothschild Family Wealth is Five Times that of World's Top 8 Billionaires Combined. The Rothschild Bloodline One of the 13 Satanic Bloodlines that Rule the World. The Rothschild Formula is soon Complete by the Economic Dismantling of the United States. Since the Rothschilds took over the Bank of England around 1815, they have been expanding their banking control over all the countries of the world. Their method has been to get a country's corrupt politicians to accept massive loans, which they can never repay, and thus go into debt to the Rothschild banking powers.

If a leader refuses to accept the loan, he is oftentimes either ousted or assassinated. And if that fails, invasions can follow, and a Rothschild usury-based bank is established. The Rothschilds exert powerful influence over the world's major news agencies too. By repetition, the masses are duped into believing horror stories about evil villains. The Rothschilds control the Bank of England, the Federal Reserve, the European Central Bank, the IMF, the World Bank and the Bank of International Settlements. Also, they own most of the gold in the world as well as the London Gold Exchange, which sets the price of gold every day. It is said the family owns over half the wealth of the planet estimated by Credit Suisse to be $231 trillion and is controlled by Evelyn Rothschild, the current head of the family.

The Illuminati and the House of Rothschild, The the illuminati" was a name used by a German sect that existed in the 15th century. They practiced the occult and professed to possess the 'light' that Lucifer had retained when he became Satan. I have been recently approached on 9/05/2018 by a GrandMaster in the Illuminati order in America he sent me this on Messenger "Join illuminati now and embrace wealthy, wealth, fame, power and protection which will help you in your life where ever you are not able to get away from it. WhatsApp the contact below if intrested +17377023469 in saying yes to all your problems" I replied him with this "Are you being serious" and he replied "Yes Brother" Watspp the grand master number on +17377023469 if you are interested in joining this great brotherhood Illuminati and for more informations." I answered "I have one question or two Is this devil worship and do I have to sell my soul to the devil" he answered "Yes you are! And in exchange our lord and master lucifer will bless you with riches, wealth, fame, money, power and protection will be given to you. But note that this great brotherhood Illuminati, does not accept any human sacrifice and hence will not ask you for such and the brotherhood does not accept blood soccer's as members. Hail the light!" I then texted back "That I was sorry but not interested and I have not heard nothing since. I wonder what their next move will be maybe to kill me because I think their must have consulted with some Wizard or Witch who could sense that I am writing about them. I hope I live long enough to see this book go live on Amazon.

In my attempt to document the origins of a secret organization which has evolved into a mastodonic nightmare, successfully creating and controlling a shadow government that supersedes several national governments, and in whose hands now lay the destiny of the world, one must carefully retrace its history.

The lengths to which this organization has gone to create the political machinery and influence public sentiment to the degree necessary to propel its self-perpetuating prophecy, are, quite frankly, mind boggling. Yet the facts provide for the undeniable truth of its existence.

Two-headed eagle emblem of the Byzantine Empire Roman Empire on a Red Shield today this is the Russian coat of arms. In 1743 a goldsmith named Amschel Moses Bauer opened a coin shop in Frankfurt, Germany. He hung above his door a sign depicting a Roman eagle on a red shield. The shop became known as the Red Shield firm. The German word for 'red shield' is Rothschild. Amschel Bauer had a son, Meyer Amschel Bauer. At a very early age Mayer showed that he possessed immense intellectual ability, and his father spent much of his time teaching him everything he could about the money lending business and in the basic dynamics of finance.

A few years after his father's death in 1755, Mayer went to work in Hannover as a clerk, in a bank, owned by the Oppenheimers. While in the employ of the Oppenheimers, he was introduced to a General von Estorff for whom he ran errands. Meyer's superior ability was quickly recognized and his advancement within the firm was swift. He was awarded a junior partnership. Von Estorff would later provide the yet-to-be formed House of Rothschild an entré into to the palace of Prince William. His success allowed him the means to return to Frankfurt and to purchase the business his father had established in 1743. The big Red Shield was still displayed over the door. Recognizing the true significance of the Red Shield his father had adopted it as his emblem from the Red Flag which was the emblem of the revolutionary minded Jews in Eastern Europe, Mayer Amschel Bauer changed his name to Rothschild red shield. It was at this point that the House of Rothschild came into being.

Through his experience with the Oppenheimers, Meyer Rothschild learned that loaning money to governments and kings was much more profitable than loaning to private individuals. Not only were the loans bigger, but they were secured by the nation's taxes. Five Sons, Five Arrows, Five Directions. Meyer Rothschild had five sons, Amschel, Salomon, Nathan, Karl and Jakob. Meyer spent the rest of his life instructing them all in the secret techniques of money creation and manipulation. As they came of age, he sent them to the major capitals of Europe to open branch offices of the family banking business. Amschel, stayed in Frankfurt, Salomon was sent to Vienna. Nathan was sent to London. Karl went to Naples, and Jakob went to Paris.

Although all the sons became astute branch managers, Nathan exhibited a superior affinity for the banking business. When he got to London, he became a merchant banker and began to cement ties between the House of Rothschild and the Bank of England. The House of Rothschild continued to buy and sell bullion and rare coins. Through their shrewd business transactions, they successfully bought out or dismantled most of the competition in Europe. In 1769, Meyer became a court agent for Prince William IX of Hesse-Kassel, who was the grandson of George II of England, a cousin to George III, a nephew of the King of Denmark, and a brother- in-law to the King of Sweden. Before long, the House of Rothschild became the go between for big Frankfurt bankers like the Bethmann Brothers, and Rueppell & Harnier.

In 1785, Meyer moved his entire family to a five-story dwelling he shared with the Schiff family. In 1865 The Schiffs' not-yet-born grandson Jacob would move to New York and in 1917 become the mastermind behind the funding of the Bolshevik Revolution. This action would successfully instate communism as a major world movement, which was, and still is, a basic tenet of the Illuminati and their collectivist agenda, from this point on the Rothschilds and the Schiffs would play a central role in the rest of European financial history, and subsequently that of the United States and the world.

Meyer Rothschild began to realize that inorder to attain the power necessary to influence and control the finances of the various monarchs in Europe, he would have to wrest this influence and power from the church, which would necessitate its destruction. To accomplish this, he enlisted the help of a Catholic priest, Adam Weishaupt, to assemble a secret Satanic order. Adam Weishaupt was born February 6, 1748 at Ingoldstadt, Bavaria. Weishaupt, born a Jew, was educated by the Jesuits who converted him to Catholicism. He purportedly developed an intense hatred for the Jesuits. Although he became a Catholic priest, his faith had been shaken by the Jesuits and he became an atheist. Weishaupt was an ardent student of French philosopher Voltaire (1694-1778). Voltaire, a revolutionary who held liberal religious views, had written in a letter to King Frederick II, ("the Great"):

"Lastly, when the whole body of the Church should be sufficiently weakened and infidelity strong enough, the final blow (is) to be dealt by the sword of open, relentless persecution. A reign of terror (is) to be spread over the whole earth, and...continue while any Christian should be found obstinate enough to adhere to Christianity."

It is believed that, as a result of Voltaire's writings, Weishaupt formulated his ideas concerning the destruction of the Church. In 1775, when summoned by the House of Rothschild, he immediately defected and, at the behest of Meyer, began to organize the Illuminati. The 1st chapter of the order started in his home town of Ingolstadt. As the name implies, those individuals who are members of the Illuminati possess the 'Light of Lucifer'. As far as they are concerned, only members of the human race who possess the 'Light of Lucifer' are truly enlightened and capable of governing. Denouncing God, Weishaupt and his followers considered themselves to be the cream of the intelligentsia the only people with the mental capacity, the knowledge, the insight and understanding necessary to govern the world and bring it peace.

Their avowed purpose and goal was the establishment of a "Novus Ordo Seclorum" a New World Order, or One World Government. Through the network of the Illuminati membership, Meyer Rothschild's efforts were redoubled, and his banking empire became firmly entrenched throughout Europe. His sons, who were made Barons of the Austrian Empire, continued to build on what their father had started and expand his financial influence.

During the American Revolution, the House of Rothschild brokered a deal between the Throne of England and Prince William of Germany. William was to provide 16,800 Hessian soldiers to help England stop the Revolution in America. Rothschild was also made responsible for the transfer of funds that were to pay the German soldiers. The transfer was never made. The soldiers were never paid, which may account for their poor showing. The Americans prevailed. At this point Meyer Rothschild set his sights on America.

LCF Rothschild Group. The Group established by Edmond de Rothschild and presided over today by his son, Benjamin, is one of the most prominent organisations in the global financial sector. LCF Rothschild Group. Meanwhile Benjamin Franklin, having become very familiar with the Bank of England and fractional reserve banking, understood the dangers of a privately owned Central Bank controlling the issue of the Nation's currency and resisted the charter of a central bank until his death in 1791. That was the same year that Alexander Hamilton pushed through legislation that would provide for the charter of The First Bank of the United States. Ironically, the bank was chartered by the Bank of England to finance the war debt of the Revolutionary War. Nathan Rothschild invested heavily in that first bank. He immediately set about to control all financial activity, between banks, in America.

There were a couple of problems, though. The U.S. Constitution put control of the nation's currency in the hands of Congress and made no provisions for Congress to delegate that authority. It even established the basic currency unit, the dollar. The dollar was Constitutionally mandated to be a silver coin based on the Spanish pillar dollar and to contain 375 grains of silver.

This single provision was designed to keep the American money supply out of the hands of the banking industry. The Bank of England made several attempts to usurp control of the U.S. money supply but failed. Still, through their Illuminati agents, they continued to enlist supporters through bribery and kickbacks. Any proponent of a fractional reserve banking system is an economic predator.

During the next twenty years the USA would fall prey to contrived financial havoc as a result of the banker's policies of creating cycles of inflation and tight money. During times of inflation the economy would boom, there would be high employment, and people would borrow money to buy houses and farms. At that point the bankers would raise interest rates and incite a depression which would, obviously, cause unemployment. People who could not pay their mortgages would have their homes and farms repossessed by the bank for a fraction of their true value. This is the essence of the Illuminati ploy, and it would recur, time and time again. In fact, it's still happening today.

By 1810, The House of Rothschild not only had a substantial stake in the Bank of the United States, they were quietly gaining control of the Bank of England. Although foreign owners were not, by law, allowed a say in the day to day operations of the Bank of the United States, there is little doubt that the American shareholders and directors were, if not affiliated, complicit in the aims and goals of the Illuminati and their central bankers.

In 1811 the charter for the First Bank of America was not renewed. As a result, the House of Rothschild lost millions. This enraged Nathan Rothschild so much that he, almost single handily fomented the War of 1812. Using his formidable power and influence, he coerced the British Parliament to attempt to retake the Colonies. The first military attempt failed. The second strategy was to divide and conquer. Any serious historian will find that the Civil War was largely stirred up by Rothschild's illuminati agents in the United States.

Meyer Amschel Rothschild died on September 19, 1812. His will spelled out specific guidelines that were to be maintained by his descendants:

1) All important posts were to be held by only family members, and only male members were to be involved on the business end. The oldest son of the oldest son was to be the head of the family, unless otherwise agreed upon by the rest of the family, as was the case in 1812, when Nathan was appointed as the patriarch.

2) The family was to intermarry with their own first and second cousins, so their fortune could be kept in the family, and to maintain the appearance of a united financial empire. For example, his son James (Jacob) Mayer married the daughter of another son, Salomon Mayer. This rule became less important in later generations as they refocused family goals and married into other fortunes.

3) Rothschild ordered that there was never to be "any public inventory made by the courts, or otherwise, of my estate...Also I forbid any legal action and any publication of the value of the inheritance."

Nathan Mayer Rothschild, who, by 1820, had established a firm grip on the Bank of England stated: "I care not what puppet is placed upon the throne of England to rule the Empire on which the sun never sets. The man who controls Britain's money supply controls the British Empire, and I control the British money supply."

The Second Bank of the United States, was also chartered by the Bank of England to carry the American war debt. When its charter expired in 1836, President Andrew Jackson refused to renew it, saying a central bank concentrated too much power in the hands of un elected bankers.

In 1838 Nathan made the following statement "Permit me to issue and control the money of a nation, and I care not who makes its laws." During the first quarter of the nineteenth century the Rothschilds expanded their financial empire throughout Europe. They crisscrossed the continent with railroads, which allowed the transport of coal and steel from their newly purchases coal mines and iron works. Through a loan to the government of England, they held the first lien on the Suez Canal. They financed the Romanov dynasty in tsarist Russia, provided the funding that allowed Cecil Rhodes the opportunity to plunder and sack Southern Africa as well as the funding that allowed the government of France to plunder and sack North Africa.

As I have stated many times before, "the Dark Side" has been on both sides of every war that has been fought in modern times. American and British Intelligence have documented evidence that the House of Rothschild has financed both sides of every war, since the American Revolution. Financier Haym Salomon, an Illuminati agent, supported the patriots during the American Revolution, then later made loans to James Madison, Thomas Jefferson, and James Monroe.

During the Napoleonic Wars, one branch of the family funded Napoleon, while another financed Great Britain, Germany, and other nations. One of the most prominent Illuminati Orders in the U.S. was the secret "Order of Skull & Bones". Illuminati agents, William Huntington Russell and Alphonso Taft, founded Chapter 322, at Yale University in 1833. Then, in 1856 the Order was incorporated as the Russell Trust.

William Russell became a member of the Connecticut State Legislature in 1846 and a General in Connecticut National Guard in 1862. Alphonso Taft became Secretary of War in the Grant Administration in 1876, U.S. Attorney General in 1876 and U.S. Ambassador to Russia in 1884. Alphonso Taft's son later became Chief Justice and United States President.

In the years preceding the Civil War, several "Skull and Bones" Patriarchs were to become leaders in the Secessionist movements of various Southern States. It has been suggested that these pressures exacerbated an already tenuous situation and set the stage for the fomentation of the Civil War. The Rothschild Banks provided financing for both the North and the South during the war. After the civil war, the cleverer method was used to take over the United States. The Rothschilds financed August Belmont, Khun Loeb and the Morgan Banks. Then they financed the Harrimans (Railroads), Carnegie (Steel) and other industrial Titans. Agents like Paul Warburg, Jacob Schiff, Bernard Baruch were then sent to the United States to affect the next phase of the takeover. By the end of the 19th. Century, the Rothschilds had controlling influence in England, U.S., France, Germany, Austria and Italy. Only Russia was left outside the financial sphere of world domination. England, through the Bank of England, ruled most of the world. Jacob Schiff, president of Khun Loeb Bank in New York was appointed by B'nai B'rith a secret Jewish Masonic Order meaning "Bothers of the Convenent" to be the Revolutionary Leader of the Revolution in Russia. A cartel, made up of the Carnegies, Morgans, Rockefellers, and Chases would contribute to the manifestation of communism.

On January 13, 1917, Leon Trotsky arrived in the United States and received a U.S. Passport. He was frequently seen entering the palatial residence of Jacob Schiff. Jacob Schiff, and his supporters, financed the training of Trotsky's Rebel Band, comprised mainly of Jews from New York's East Side, on Rockefeller's Standard Oil Company property in New Jersey.

When sufficiently trained in the techniques of guerrilla warfare and terror, Trotsky's rebel band departed with twenty million dollars' worth of gold, also provided by Jacob Schiff, on the ship S.S. Kristianiafjord bound for Russia to wage the Bolshevik revolution. After the Bolshevik Revolution and the wholesale murder of the entire Russian royal family, Standard Oil of New Jersey brought 50% of the huge Caucasus oil field even though the property had theoretically been nationalized. In 1927, Standard Oil of New York built a refinery in Russia.

Then Standard Oil concluded a deal to market Soviet Oil in Europe and floated a loan of $75 million to the Bolsheviks. Jacob Schiff and Paul Warburg at the Kuhn Loeb Bank started a campaign for a central bank in the United States. They then helped the Rothschild's to manipulate the financial Panic of 1907.

Then, the panic of 1907 was used as an argument for having a central bank to prevent such occurrences. Paul Warburg told the Banking and Currency Committee: 'Let us have a national clearing house'. The Federal Reserve Act was the brainchild of Baron Alfred Rothschild of London. The final version of the Act was decided on at a secret meeting at Jekyll Island Georgia, owned by J.P. Morgan. Present at the meeting were; A. Piatt Andrew, Assistant secretary of the Treasury, Senator Nelson Aldrich, Frank Vanderlip, President of Kuhn Loeb and Co., Henry Davidson, Senior Partner of J.P. Morgan Bank, Charles Norton, President of Morgan's First National of New York, Paul Warburg, Partner in Khun Loeb and Co. and Benjamin Strong, President of Morgan's Bankers Trust Co. The Federal Reserve Act of 1913, brought about the decimation of the U.S. Constitution and was the determining act of the international financiers in consolidating financial power in the United States. Pierre Jay, initiated into the "Order of Skull and Bones" in 1892, became the first Chairman of the New York Federal Reserve Bank. A dozen members of the Federal Reserve can be linked to the same "Order."

The Rothschilds operate out of an area in the heart of London, England, the financial district, which is known as 'The City ', or the 'Square Mile.' All major British banks have their main offices here, along with branch offices for 385 foreign banks, including 70 from the United States.

It is here that you will find the Bank of England, the Stock Exchange, Lloyd's of London, the Baltic Exchange shipping contracts, Fleet Street home of publishing and newspaper interests, the London Commodity Exchange to trade coffee, rubber, sugar and wool, and the London Metal Exchange. It is virtually the financial hub of the world.

Positioned on the north bank of the Thames River, covering an area of 677 acres or one square mile (known as the "wealthiest square mile on earth"), it has enjoyed special rights and privileges that enabled them to achieve a certain level of independence since 1191. In 1215, its citizens received a Charter from King John, granting them the right to annually elect a Mayor known as the Lord Mayor, a tradition that continues today.

Des Griffin, in his book Descent into Slavery, described 'The City' as a sovereign state much like the Vatican, and that since the establishment of the privately-owned Bank of England in 1694, this financial center has actually become the last word in England's national affairs. He contends that the country is run by powers in 'the City' and that the throne, the prime minister, and parliament are simply fronts for the real power. E. C. Knuth, in his book Empire of the City, suggests that when the queen enters 'The City,' she is subservient to the Lord Mayor under him, is a committee of 12-14 men, known as 'The Crown', because this privately-owned corporation is not subject to the Queen, or the Parliament. The Rothschilds have traditionally chosen the Lord mayor since 1820.

The last national election in the United States provided its citizenry with a choice between two known members of the same Satanic cult. And even then, the outcome of this election has come under extreme scrutiny. It has been said that those who vote decide nothing and those who count the vote decide everything. The French Revolution of 1789-1799 was a fight not only against feudalism and the French monarchy, but also against the Church. The Word of God was replaced with the goddess of Reason. God's standard was replaced with a human standard: The Declaration of the Rights of Man and of the Citizen. The French Revolution and the spread of the antiChristian Cult of Reason were the result of Jesuit, Masonic, and Illuminati influence. The Phrygian cap, used as a symbol of freedom by the Jacobins in the French Revolution. This cap is really Mithra's cap. Mithraism is expressed in Roman Catholicism today. The Phrygian cap, used as a symbol of freedom by the Jacobins in the French.

When Jesuit Professor Adam Weishaupt created the Order of the Illuminati in 1776 in Bavaria, Germany. These Illuminati were part of the coalition of rebels that became the Jacobins the group responsible for the French Revolution.

The Jacobins terrorized France, Barruel arguments in his preface, could not have appeared out of thin air. The principal authors of the conspiracy, he claimed, were Voltaire, Jean-le-Rond d'Alembert, and King Frederick of Prussia, who had secretly planned to destroy Christianity. These "sophists" had formed an alliance with the Freemasons, whose antireligious conspirator origins Barruel traced back to the medieval Knights Templars. The final and most utterly evil group in this triple conspiracy, however, were the Bavarian Illuminati, under their satanic leader Adam Weishaupt.

Jacobinism had emerged out of the union of these three groups. The French philosopher Voltaire, whose ideas were instrumental in the French Revolution, was a Freemason as was Napoleon too. The evidence in favour of a Masonic initiation before Napoleon's assumption of the imperial title is overwhelming.

American historian Emanuel Josephson tells us that the Jesuits used Napoleon in their larger scheme, Weishaupt and his fellow Jesuits whose income had been stopped by the Vatican, launched and lead the French Revolution by directing Napoleon's conquest of Catholic Europe; by eventually having Napoleon throw Pope Pius VII into jail at Avignon until he agreed, as the price of his release, to re-establish the Jesuit Order. This Jesuit war on the Vatican was terminated by the Congress of Vienna and by the secret, 1822, Treaty of Verona.

Eric Phelps explains that "The parallels between the Jesuits' French and Russian Revolutions are striking." Here are some of the comparisons:

1. Both revolutions were based on communist writings of Freemasons Voltaire and Marx. Did not the Jesuits perfect communism on their reductions in Paraguay?

2. Both revolutions plundered the state churches.

3. Both revolutions ended the monarchies. We're not the Jesuits enemies of both the Bourbon and the Romanoff dynasties? Had not both monarchies expelled the Jesuits from their countries?

4. Both revolutions produced Jesuit Republics in form, but absolute monarchies in power.

5. Both revolutions declared atheism as the religion of the state. Evidenced by their deeds, are not the Jesuits truly atheists?

6. Both revolutions carried out a reign of terror by some inquisitional secret police.

7. Both revolutions resulted in military dictators who punished the enemies of the Jesuits. Did not the Jesuits benefit even though Napoleon and Stalin, in deceiving the nations, openly banned the Order from France and Russia?

During the Order's Suppression from 1773 to 1814 by Pope Clement XIV, General Ricci created the Illuminati with his soldier, Adam Weishaupt, the Father of modern Communism, who, with his Jacobins, conducted the French Revolution. Years later Jesuit General Ledochowski, with his Bolsheviks, conducted the Russian Revolution in 1917, it being identical to the upheaval of 1789 French revolution.

Freemasonry started in Europe sometime around the 16th century, and now is a network of at least six million "brothers" around the world. Many if not all-American presidents have been involved in Masonry. Although some parts of Freemasonry are secret, this society is really a front organization controlled by the Society of Jesus the Jesuits. If you trace up Masonry, through all its Orders, till you come to the grand tip-top, head Mason of the World, you will discover that the dread individual and the Chief of the Society of Jesus are one and the same person! The truth is, the Jesuits of Rome have perfected Freemasonry to be their most magnificent and effective tool, accomplishing their purposes among Protestants.

Even members of the New Age movement recognize this connection. Theosophist Helena Blavatsky says this "It is curious to note too that most of the bodies which work these, such as the Ancient and Accepted Scottish Rite, the Rite of Avignon, the Order of the Temple, Fessler's Rite, the "Grand Council of the Emperors of the East and West "Sovereign Prince Masons," etc., etc., are nearly all the offspring of the sons of Ignatius Loyola. The Baron Hundt, Chevalier Ramsay, Tschoudy, Zinnendorf, and numerous others who founded the grades in these rites, worked under instructions from the General of the Jesuits. The nest where these high degrees were hatched, and no Masonic rite is free from their baleful influence more or less, was the Jesuit College of Clermont at Paris. Freemasonry carries on the legacy of the Knights Templar, a military order controlled by the Pope.

Although the Knights Templar supposedly do not exist in the same form, a group associated with Freemasonry called the Knights Templar does still exist, and similar organizations such as the Knights of Malta also carry on the legacy. Some Secret Knowledge is meant to be shared amongst all Freemasons, the highest levels of Freemasonry have the Gnostic "secret knowledge" that they hide from the rest of the world, and even lower-level Masons are kept in the dark. There is a division between the inner circle and the outer, the freemen who have the knowledge, and the commoners who don't even know they are being controlled and enslaved too.

"We must create a super rite, which will remain unknown, to which we will call those Masons of high degree (30th and above), whom we shall select. With regards to our brothers in Masonry, these men must be pledged to the strictest secrecy. Through this supreme rite, we will govern all Freemasonry which will become the one international centre the more powerful, because its direction will be unknown."

The Blue Degrees are but the outer court of portico of the Temple. Part of the symbols are displayed there to the Initiate, but he is intentionally misled by false interpretations. It is not intended that he shall understand them; but it is intended that he shall imagine he understands them. Their true explication is reserved for the Adepts, the Princes of Masonry. The whole body of the Royal and Sacerdotal Art was hidden so carefully, centuries since, in the High Degrees.

Since the beginning, the purpose of the Jesuits has included global political domination, as Loyola himself once said "Finally, Let all with such artfulness gain the ascendant over princes, noblemen, and the magistrates of every place, that they may be ready at our beck, even to sacrifice their nearest relations and most intimate friends, when we say it is for our interest and advantage" At what then do the Jesuits aim? According to them, they only seek the greater glory of God; but if you examine the facts you will find that they aim at universal dominion alone. They have rendered themselves indispensable to the Pope, who, without them, could not exist, because Catholicism is identified with them. They have rendered themselves indispensable to governors and hold revolutions in their hands; and in this way, either under one name or another, it is they who rule the world. As the sources below attest, the Jesuits have been involved in and even spearheaded many of the world's worst wars, revolutions, and massacres. At times, the Jesuits are directly involved, at other times, they use their influence over the Freemasons and other secret societies.

The Ustaša Military Organisation the Papacy's connections with the Croation Ustaše were obvious from the beginning as top Serb civilians were forced to convert to Catholicism by the Ustaše in Glina. In 1929, the Ustaša military organization was founded. This group assassinated King Alexander of Yugoslavia in 1934, and slaughtered Jewish and Orthodox Croatians. For the Ustaša, "relations with the Vatican were as important as relations with Germany."

In 1941, Adolf Hitler put the Ustasha into power, in compliance with the Vatican-Third Reich Concordat, of July 20, 1933. Under that Concordat Dr. Ante Pavelic, the dictator of Croatia with the direct aid of the Archbishop of Zagreb Cardinal Alojzije Stepinac instructed the Ustasha to implement a program of forced "conversion" of the Croatia population to Catholicism 840,000 people were murdered when they refused to become Roman Catholics.

In an official document dated as late as May 8, 1944, His Eminence Archbishop Stepinac, head of the Catholic hierarchy in Nazi Croatia, who was later convicted of war crimes informed the Holy Father that to date '244,000 Orthodox Serbs have been converted to the Church of God. "You must consider the fact that the Orthodox Churches image of Christ is of African origin too. Catholic priest and writer Franjo Kralik wrote this in the Croation version of Catholic Weekly in 1941 "Love has its limits. The movement for freeing the world from the Jews is a movement for the renaissance of human dignity. The all wise and Almighty God is behind this movement."

World War II began because Hitler approved of everything particularly relating to Jesuit Catholicism as opposed to Protestantism. He approved of the indisputability of Catholic dogmas, of the intolerant attitude of Catholic education, of the necessity of blind faith, of the personal infallibility of the Pope...In an open and prophetic expression of his admiration for the Catholic Church, he says: "Thus the Catholic Church is more secure than ever. It can be predicted that, as passing phenomena vanish away, she will remain as a beacon light" One of the principle Catholic personalities to help Hitler into power was Franz von Papen, leader of the Catholic Party in Germany and friend of Pacelli. Hitler himself said this "I learned much from the order of the Jesuits...Until now there has never been anything more grandiose, on the earth, than the hierarchical system of the catholic church. I transferred much of this organization into my own party."

The powerful Nazi leader Franz von Papen, Vice-Chancellor of the Reich, said this "The Third Reich is the first world power which not only acknowledges but also puts into practice the high principles of the papacy" In response to von Papen's surprising claims, historian P. D. Stuart asks, "Now, are we to regard it as sheer coincidence that von Papen was not only Vice-Chancellor of the Nazi party, but also a member of the Catholic Center Party in the parliament of the Weimar Republic (1919-1933)? And is it merely coincidental that von Papen was also given the honorary dignity (title) of Papal Chamberlain by Pope Pius XI; or that the said honour was revived on July 24, 1959 by Pope John XXIII?"

Note, as an aside, that the Third Reich was not the only superpower to follow the Pope's principles. American President George W. Bush called John Paul II, "a champion of human freedom" and "an inspiration to millions of Americans." In 2001 the Bush-appointed US ambassador to the Vatican declared that the "values of the Bush Administration and those of the Vatican line up hand in glove."

Chief of the Nazi Sicherheitdienst Walter Shellenberg tells us about the Nazi secret service "The SS had been organized by Heinrich Himmler according to the principles of the Jesuit Order. The rules of service and spiritual exercises prescribed by Ignatius de Loyola constituted a model which Heinrich Himmler strove carefully to copy. Absolute obedience was the supreme rule; every order had to be executed without comment." Himmler was closely associated with the Jesuits through his father and brother. Hitler said of him, "I can see Himmler as our Ignatius of Loyola."

P. D. Stuart questions these connections, as should we too, why were Hitler's closest advisers Jesuits? Why did Mr Adolf Hitler admire and copy the Jesuits? Are these just mere coincidences? Or are we once again seeing the Jesuits playing the chameleon, and eclipsing the wiles of Ovid? Let us not mince words here, Hitler, the faithful "son of the Catholic Church," was the Pope's Malleus Papa his hammer.

Fidel Castro's time in power was also part of the Jesuit ploy. Wherever a totalitarian movement erupts, whether Communist or Nazism or fascism, a Jesuit can be found in the role of "adviser" or leader; in Cuba it was Castro's "Father" Armando Llorente. Castro himself was Jesuit-trained at various Jesuit schools, including El Colegio de Belén, a Jesuit boarding school in Havana!

Zimbabwe's president Robert Mugabe, leader of Africa's long running "reign of terror," has Jesuitical roots. Robert Mugabe is also Jesuit trained. Mugabe was raised as a Roman Catholic, studied in Marxist and Jesuit schools, including the exclusive Kutama College, headed by Father Jerome O'Hea, S.J., who took Mugabe under his wing. Lord David Owen, British Foreign Secretary in the late 1970s, has this to say about Mugabe "Whatever Robert Mugabe, Zimbabwe's leader, may claim in the coming days, there is no way that the country can have anything like fair and free elections. His ruthlessness became clear to me when, as Foreign Secretary, I was negotiating with him over Rhodesian independence between 1977 and 1979" ...

He was, however, an ideological zealot of Jesuit upbringing, implacable and obdurate." The Papacy and the Jesuit Order were behind Mugabe and his seemingly "unCatholic" actions. Amid escalating calls to excommunicate him from the Roman Catholic Church, President Robert Mugabe had donated large sums of money to it. Father Oskar Wermter, a Jesuit missionary priest who has lived in Zimbabwe for over 30 years, said calls to excommunicate Mugabe were "old hat" and were unlikely to be heard. Many writers have tried warning us of the great conspiracy of the Jesuits. Samuel Morse, the father of Morse Code, was one of them. The preface of Foreign Conspiracy Against the Liberties of the United States, written in 1835, reads as follows Samuel Morse in 1840.

"The author undertakes to show that a conspiracy against the liberties of this Republic is now in full action, under the direction of the wily Prince Metternich of Austria, who knowing the impossibility of obliterating this troublesome example of a great and free nation by force of arms, is attempting to accomplish his object through the agency of an army of Jesuits. The array of facts and arguments going to prove the existence of such a conspiracy, will astonish any man who opens the book with the same incredulity as we did."In 1816 John Adams wrote this to President Jefferson "Shall we not have regular swarms of them here, in as many disguises as only a king of the gypsies can assume, dressed as painters, publishers, writers and schoolmasters? If ever there was a body of men who merited eternal damnation on earth and in hell it is this Society of Loyola's." President Abraham Lincoln said this "The Protestants of both the North and South would surely unite to exterminate the priests and the Jesuits, if they could learn how the priests, the nuns, and the monks, which daily land on our shores, under the pretext of preaching their religion are nothing else but the emissaries of the Pope, of Napoleon III, and the other despots of Europe, to undermine our institutions, alienate the hearts of our people from our constitution, and our laws, destroy our schools, and prepare a reign of anarchy here as they have done in Ireland, in Mexico, in Spain, and wherever there are any people who want to be free."

The great French General Marquis de Lafayette once said this "It is my opinion that if the liberties of this country the United States of America are destroyed, it will be by the subtlety of the Roman Catholic Jesuit priests, for they are the most crafty, dangerous enemies to civil and religious liberty. They have instigated most of the wars of Europe." These men of the past knew the truth.

As we can see by the list below, many American universities are run by Jesuits. Frighteningly, American presidents are being trained at these institutions, along with many other high government officials.

In the case of the Boer War, the motivating factor was two-fold, firstly, the Boer states were sat on top of one of the largest gold deposits on the globe, with the extra benefit of their being lots of diamonds and other precious minerals. Secondly, the Boers were a group of Europeans (Dutch Calvanists, French Heugenots, German Protestants) who had turned their back on the established order and had established for themselves an independent homeland outside of the global financial system, they had a government owned and controlled central bank that issued debt-free currency backed by gold, which meant they had zero inflation and zero interest on credit. Quite obviously, such a state and financial system is diametrically opposed to how the banking systems of all other countries work at the time of the Boer War, both Britain and the US had currencies backed by gold but neither had a state-owned and controlled central bank and was not acceptable to the international bankers who control the world The Rothschilds and their partners/vassals.

It was no secret that Cecil Rhodes worked for the Rothschilds and they were the ones who financed all of his murderous, grandiose plans for imperial conquest and exploitation of native peoples. Therefore, the Boer war is a straightforward case of an agent of the Rothschilds using Rothschild money to arm a group of mercenary terrorists then sending these gangsters to attack a state from the inside thus provoking war between the state and the state controlled by the Rothschilds (Britain). It is no secret that the Rothschilds loaned the British Government money to finance the war so the 1 million British and Empire troops who served in South Africa were effectively mercenaries hired and paid for by the Rothschilds.

Hundreds of thousands of soldiers and civilians died as a result, no-one knows how many Boer civilians died, but at least 30,000 died in the British concentration camps alone, no-one knows how many were killed on their own farms and homesteads. Therefore, my study of the Boer War led me to understand how wars are planned, organised, provoked and financed, and who is behind this evil mechanism that slaughters innocent people in-masse to funnel all of the world's gold into the hands of a handful of families who control the world's financial system. You can take the pattern I just explained and apply it to almost any conflict since the Boer War, it will fit like a glove.

The Rothschild family is slowly but surely having their Central banks established in every country of this world, giving them incredible amount of wealth and power. In the year of 2000 there were seven countries without a Rothschild owned or controlled Central Bank: Afghanistan; Iraq; Sudan; Libya; Cuba; North Korea and Iran. It is not a coincidence that these country, which are listed above were and are still being under attack by the western media, since one of the main reasons these countries have been under attack in the first place is because they do not have a Rothschild owned Central Bank yet.

The family has been around for more than 230 years and has slithered its way into each country on this planet, threatened every world leader and their governments and cabinets with physical and economic death and destruction, and then emplaced their own people in these central banks to control and manage each country's pocketbook.

Worse, the Rothschilds also control the machinations of each government at the macro level, not concerning themselves with the daily vicissitudes of our individual personal lives. Except when we get too far out of line. The Attacks of September 11th were an inside job to invade Afghanistan and Iraq to then establish a Central Bank in those countries. After the instigated protests and riots in the Arab countries the Rothschild finally paved their way into establishing Central Banks, and getting rid of many leaders, which put them into more power.

Complete List of BANKS Owned or Controlled by the Rothschild Family (As of 2013)

Afghanistan: Bank of Afghanistan

Albania: Bank of Albania

Algeria: Bank of Algeria

Argentina: Central Bank of Argentina

Armenia: Central Bank of Armenia

Aruba: Central Bank of Aruba

Australia: Reserve Bank of Australia

Austria: Austrian National Bank

Azerbaijan: Central Bank of Azerbaijan Republic

Bahamas: Central Bank of The Bahamas

Bahrain: Central Bank of Bahrain

Bangladesh: Bangladesh Bank

Barbados: Central Bank of Barbados

Belarus: National Bank of the Republic of Belarus

Belgium: National Bank of Belgium

Belize: Central Bank of Belize

Benin: Central Bank of West African States (BCEAO)

Bermuda: Bermuda Monetary Authority

Bhutan: Royal Monetary Authority of Bhutan

Bolivia: Central Bank of Bolivia

Bosnia: Central Bank of Bosnia and Herzegovina

Botswana: Bank of Botswana

Brazil: Central Bank of Brazil

Bulgaria: Bulgarian National Bank

Burkina Faso: Central Bank of West African States (BCEAO)

Burundi: Bank of the Republic of Burundi

Cambodia: National Bank of Cambodia

Came Roon: Bank of Central African States

Canada: Bank of Canada – Banque du Canada

Cayman Islands: Cayman Islands Monetary Authority

Central African Republic: Bank of Central African States

Chad: Bank of Central African States

Chile: Central Bank of Chile

China: The People's Bank of China

Colombia: Bank of the Republic

Comoros: Central Bank of Comoros

Congo: Bank of Central African States

Costa Rica: Central Bank of Costa Rica

Côte d'Ivoire: Central Bank of West African States (BCEAO)

Croatia: Croatian National Bank

Cuba: Central Bank of Cuba

Cyprus: Central Bank of Cyprus

Czech Republic: Czech National Bank

Denmark: National Bank of Denmark

Dominican Republic: Central Bank of the Dominican Republic

East Caribbean area: Eastern Caribbean Central Bank

Ecuador: Central Bank of Ecuador

Egypt: Central Bank of Egypt

El Salvador: Central Reserve Bank of El Salvador

Equatorial Guinea: Bank of Central African States

Estonia: Bank of Estonia

Ethiopia: National Bank of Ethiopia

European Union: European Central Bank

Fiji: Reserve Bank of Fiji

Finland: Bank of Finland

France: Bank of France

Gabon: Bank of Central African States

The Gambia: Central Bank of The Gambia

Georgia: National Bank of Georgia

Germany: Deutsche Bundesbank

Ghana: Bank of Ghana

Greece: Bank of Greece

Guatemala: Bank of Guatemala

Guinea Bissau: Central Bank of West African States (BCEAO)

Guyana: Bank of Guyana

Haiti: Central Bank of Haiti

Honduras: Central Bank of Honduras

Hong Kong: Hong Kong Monetary Authority

Hungary: Magyar Nemzeti Bank

Iceland: Central Bank of Iceland

India: Reserve Bank of India

Indonesia: Bank Indonesia

Iran: The Central Bank of the Islamic Republic of Iran

Iraq: Central Bank of Iraq

Ireland: Central Bank and Financial Services Authority of Ireland

Israel: Bank of Israel

Italy: Bank of Italy

Jamaica: Bank of Jamaica

Japan: Bank of Japan

Jordan: Central Bank of Jordan

Kazakhstan: National Bank of Kazakhstan

Kenya: Central Bank of Kenya

Korea: Bank of Korea

Kuwait: Central Bank of Kuwait

Kyrgyzstan: National Bank of the Kyrgyz Republic

Latvia: Bank of Latvia

Lebanon: Central Bank of Lebanon

Lesotho: Central Bank of Lesotho

Libya: Central Bank of Libya (Their most recent conquest)

Uruguay: Central Bank of Uruguay

Lithuania: Bank of Lithuania

Luxembourg: Central Bank of Luxembourg

Macao: Monetary Authority of Macao

Macedonia: National Bank of the Republic of Macedonia

Madagascar: Central Bank of Madagascar

Malawi: Reserve Bank of Malawi

Malaysia: Central Bank of Malaysia

Mali: Central Bank of West African States (BCEAO)

Malta: Central Bank of Malta

Mauritius: Bank of Mauritius

Mexico: Bank of Mexico

Moldova: National Bank of Moldova

Mongolia: Bank of Mongolia

Montenegro: Central Bank of Montenegro

Morocco: Bank of Morocco

Mozambique: Bank of Mozambique

Namibia: Bank of Namibia

Nepal: Central Bank of Nepal

Netherlands: Netherlands Bank

Netherlands Antilles: Bank of the Netherlands Antilles

New Zealand: Reserve Bank of New Zealand

Nicaragua: Central Bank of Nicaragua

Niger: Central Bank of West African States (BCEAO)

Nigeria: Central Bank of Nigeria

Norway: Central Bank of Norway

Oman: Central Bank of Oman

Pakistan: State Bank of Pakistan

Papua New Guinea: Bank of Papua New Guinea

Paraguay: Central Bank of Paraguay

Peru: Central Reserve Bank of Peru

Philip Pines: Bangko Sentral ng Pilipinas

Poland: National Bank of Poland

Portugal: Bank of Portugal

Qatar: Qatar Central Bank

Romania: National Bank of Romania

Russia: Central Bank of Russia

Rwanda: National Bank of Rwanda

San Marino: Central Bank of the Republic of San Marino

Samoa: Central Bank of Samoa

Saudi Arabia: Saudi Arabian Monetary Agency

Senegal: Central Bank of West African States (BCEAO)

Serbia: National Bank of Serbia

Seychelles: Central Bank of Seychelles

Sierra Leone: Bank of Sierra Leone

Singapore: Monetary Authority of Singapore

Slovakia: National Bank of Slovakia

Slovenia: Bank of Slovenia

Solomon Islands: Central Bank of Solomon Islands

South Africa: South African Reserve Bank

Spain: Bank of Spain

Sri Lanka: Central Bank of Sri Lanka

Sudan: Bank of Sudan

Surinam: Central Bank of Suriname

Swaziland: The Central Bank of Swaziland

Sweden: Sveriges Riksbank

Switzerland: Swiss National Bank

Tajikistan: National Bank of Tajikistan

Tanzania: Bank of Tanzania

Thailand: Bank of Thailand

Togo: Central Bank of West African States (BCEAO)

Tonga: National Reserve Bank of Tonga

Trinidad and Tobago: Central Bank of Trinidad and Tobago

Tunisia: Central Bank of Tunisia

Turkey: Central Bank of the Republic of Turkey

Uganda: Bank of Uganda

Ukraine: National Bank of Ukraine

United Arab Emirates: Central Bank of United Arab Emirates

United Kingdom: Bank of England

United States: Federal Reserve, Federal Reserve Bank of New York

Vanuatu: Reserve Bank of Vanuatu

Venezuela: Central Bank of Venezuela

Vietnam: The State Bank of Vietnam

Yemen: Central Bank of Yemen

Zambia: Bank of Zambia

Zimbabwe: Reserve Bank of Zimbabwe

Virtually unknown to the general public is the fact that the US Federal Reserve is a privately-owned company, siting on its very own patch of land, immune to the US laws. This privately-owned company controlled by the Rothschild's, Rockefeller's and Morgan's prints the money for the US Government, which pays them interest for the "favour." This means that if we would reset the nation's debt today and would begin reprinting money, we would be in debt to the FED from the very first dollar loaned to our Government. Most people living in the USA have no clue that the Internal Revenue Service (IRS) is a foreign agency. To be more accurate, the IRS is a foreign private corporation of the International Monetary Fund (IMF) and is the private "army" of the Federal Reserve (Fed). Its main goal is to make sure the American people pay their tax and be good little slaves.

Rothschilds Want Iran's Banks could be gaining control of the Central Bank of the Islamic Republic of Iran (CBI) be one of the main reasons that Iran is being targeted by Western and Israeli powers? As tensions are building up for an unthinkable war with Iran, it is worth exploring Iran's banking system compared to its U.S., British and Israeli counterparts. Some researchers are pointing out that Iran is one of only three countries left in the world whose central bank is not under Rothschild control. Before 9-11 there were reportedly seven: Afghanistan, Iraq, Sudan, Libya, Cuba, North Korea and Iran. By 2003, however, Afghanistan and Iraq were swallowed up by the Rothschild octopus, and by 2011 Sudan and Libya were also gone. In Libya, a Rothschild bank was established in Benghazi while the country was still at war.

Islam forbids the charging of interest, a major problem for the Rothschild banking system. Until a few hundred years ago, charging interest was also forbidden in the Christian world and was even punishable by death. It was considered exploitation and enslavement.

Causes of Wars in Africa,

There is a very simple reason why some of Africa's bloodiest, most brutal wars never seem to end, they are not really wars. Not in the traditional sense, at least. These combatants don't have much of an ideology and they don't have clear goals. They couldn't care less about taking over capitals or major cities in fact, they prefer the deep bush, where it is far easier to commit crimes. Today's rebels seem especially uninterested in winning converts, content instead to steal other people's children, stick Kalashnikovs or axes in their hands, and make them do the killing. Look closely at some of the continent's most intractable conflicts, from the rebel-laden creeks of the Niger Delta to the inferno in the Democratic Republic of the Congo, and this is what you will find. What we are seeing is the decline of the classic African liberation movement and the proliferation of something else something wilder, messier, more violent, and harder to wrap our heads around. What is spreading across Africa like a viral pandemic is actually just opportunistic, heavily armed banditry.

Most of today's African fighters are not rebels with a cause, they're just predators why can't the lay down the arms and talk peacefully. That's why we see stunning atrocities like eastern Congo's rape epidemic, where armed groups in recent years have sexually assaulted hundreds of thousands of women, often so sadistically that the victims are left incontinent for life. What is the military or political objective of ramming an assault rifle inside a woman and pulling the trigger? Terror has become an end, not just a means. This is the story across much of Africa, where nearly half of the continent's 53 countries are home to an active conflict or a recently ended one. Quiet places such as Tanzania are the lonely exceptions; even user-friendly, tourist-filled Kenya blew up in 2008. More than 5 million have died in Congo alone since 1998, the International Rescue Committee has estimated.

Of course, many of the last generation's independence struggles were bloody, too. South Sudan's decades-long rebellion is thought to have cost more than 2 million lives. But this is not about numbers. This is about methods and objectives, and the leaders driving them. Uganda's top guerrilla of the 1980s, Yoweri Museveni, used to fire up his rebels by telling them they were on the ground floor of a national people's army. Museveni became president in 1986, and he's still in office another problem.

But his words seem downright noble compared with the best-known rebel leader from his country today, Joseph Kony, who just gives orders to burn. Even if you could coax these men out of their jungle lairs and get them to the negotiating table, there is very little to offer them. They don't want ministries or tracts of land to govern. Their armies are often traumatized children, with no experience and skills they are totally unsuited for civilian life. All they want is cash, guns, and a license to rampage. How do you negotiate with that?

The short answer is you don't. The only way to stop today's rebels for real is to capture or kill their leaders. Many are uniquely devious characters whose organizations would likely disappear as soon as they do. That's what happened in Angola when the diamond-smuggling rebel leader Jonas Savimbi was shot, bringing a sudden end to one of the Cold War's most intense conflicts. In Liberia, the moment that warlord-turned-president Charles Taylor was arrested in 2006 was the same moment that the curtain dropped on the gruesome circus of 10-year-old killers wearing Halloween masks. Countless dollars, hours, and lives have been wasted on fruitless rounds of talks that will never culminate in such clear-cut results.

The same could be said of indictments of rebel leaders for crimes against humanity by the International Criminal Court. With the prospect of prosecution looming, those fighting are sure never to give up. How did we get here? Maybe it's pure nostalgia, but it seems that yesteryear's African rebels had a bit more class. They were fighting against colonialism, tyranny, or apartheid. The winning insurgencies often came with a charming, intelligent leader wielding persuasive rhetoric. These were men like John Garang, who led the rebellion in southern Sudan with his Sudan People's Liberation Army. He pulled off what few guerrilla leaders anywhere have done: winning his people their own country.

Thanks in part to his tenacity, South Sudan will held a referendum to secede from the North. Garang died in a 2005 helicopter crash, but people still talk about him like a god. Unfortunately, the region without him looks pretty godforsaken. Even Robert Mugabe's, Zimbabwe's dictatorship, was once a guerrilla with a plan. After transforming minority white-run Rhodesia into majority black-run Zimbabwe, he turned his country into one of the fastest-growing and most diversified economies south of the Sahara for the first decade and a half of his rule.

His status as a true war hero, and the aid he lent other African liberation movements in the 1980s, account for many African leaders' reluctance to criticize him today, even as he has led Zimbabwe down a path straight to hell. These men are living relics of a past that has been essentially obliterated. Put the well-educated Garang and the old Mugabe in a room with today's visionless rebel leaders, and they would have just about nothing in common. What changed in one generation was in part the world itself. The Cold War's end bred state collapse and chaos. Where meddling great powers once found dominoes that needed to be kept from falling, they suddenly saw no national interest at all. The exceptions for the need for war's, of course, were natural resources, which could be bought just as easily and often at a nice discount from various armed groups. Suddenly, all you needed to be powerful was a gun, and as it turned out, there were plenty to go around. AK-47s and cheap ammunition bled out of the collapsed Eastern Bloc and into the farthest corners of Africa. It was the perfect opportunity for the charismatic and morally challenged.

In Congo, there have been dozens of such men since 1996, when rebels revolted against the leopard skin-capped dictator Mobutu Sese Seko, probably the most corrupt man in the history of this most corrupt continent. After Mobutu's state collapsed, no one really rebuilt it. In the anarchy that flourished, rebel leaders carved out fiefdoms ludicrously rich in gold, diamonds, copper, tin, and other minerals. Among them were Laurent Nkunda, Bosco Ntaganda, Thomas Lubanga, a toxic hodgepodge of Mai Mai commanders, Rwandan genocidaires, and the madman leaders of a flamboyantly cruel group called the Rastas. Nkunda is not totally wrong about Congo's mess. Ethnic tensions are a real piece of the conflict, together with disputes over land, refugees, and meddling neighbouring countries.

But what I've come to understand is how quickly legitimate grievances in these failed or failing African states deteriorate into rapacious, profit-oriented for arms dealers worldwide. Congo today is home to a resource rebellion in which vague anti-government feelings become an excuse to steal public property. Congo's embarrassment of riches belongs to the 70 million Congolese, but in the past 10 to 15 years, that treasure has been hijacked by a couple dozen rebel commanders who use it to buy even more guns and wreak more havoc. Probably the most disturbing example of an African un-war comes from the Lord's Resistance Army (LRA), begun as a rebel movement in northern Uganda during the lawless 1980s.

Like the gangs in the oil-polluted Niger Delta, the LRA at first had some legitimate grievances namely, the poverty and marginalization of the country's ethnic Acholi areas. The movement's leader, Joseph Kony, was a young, wig-wearing, gibberish-speaking, so-called prophet who espoused the Ten Commandments. Soon, he broke everyone. He used his supposed magic powers and drugs to whip his followers into a frenzy and unleashed them on the very Acholi people he was supposed to be protecting.

The LRA literally carved their way across the region, leaving a trail of hacked-off limbs and sawed-off ears. They don't talk about the Ten Commandments anymore, and some of those left in their wake can barely talk at all. When Uganda finally got its act together in the late 1990s and cracked down, Kony and his men simply marched on. Today, their scourge has spread to one of the world's most lawless regions: the borderland where Sudan, Congo, and the Central African Republic meet. Child soldiers are an inextricable part of these movements. The LRA, for example, never seize territory they seize children. Its ranks are filled with brainwashed boys and girls who ransack villages and who pound new-born babies to death with wooden mortars. In Congo, as many as one-third of all combatants are under age of 18. Since the new predatory style of African warfare is motivated and financed by crime, popular support is irrelevant to these rebels. The downside to not caring about winning hearts and minds, though, is that you don't win many recruits. So, abducting and manipulating children becomes the only way to sustain the organized banditry. And children have turned out to be ideal weapons easily brainwashed, intensely loyal, fearless, and, most importantly, in endless supply.

In this new age of forever wars, even Somalia looks different. That country certainly evokes the image of Africa's most chaotic state exceptional even in its neighbourhood for unending conflict. But what if Somalia is less of an outlier than a terrifying forecast of what war in Africa is moving toward? On the surface, Somalia seems wracked by a religiously themed civil conflict between the internationally backed but feckless transitional government and the Islamist militia al-Shabab.

Yet the fighting is being nourished by the same old Somali problem that has dogged this desperately poor country since 1991, warlords many of which are the men who command or fund militias in Somalia today are the same ones who tore the place apart over the past 20 years in a scramble for the few resources left the port, airport, telephone poles, and grazing pastures.

Somalis are getting sick of the Shabab and its draconian rules of no music, no gold teeth, even no bras. But what has kept locals in Somalia from revolting against foreign terrorists is Somalia's deeply ingrained culture of war profiteering. Many powerful Somalis have a vested interest in the status quo chaos. One olive oil exporter in Mogadishu stated that he and some trader friends bought a crate of missiles to shoot at government soldiers because "taxes are annoying." Most frightening is how many sick states like Congo are now showing Somalia-like symptoms. Whenever a potential leader emerges to reimpose order in Mogadishu, criminal networks rise up to finance his opponent, no matter who that may be. The longer these areas are stateless, the harder it is to go back to the necessary evil of government. All this might seem a gross simplification, and indeed, not all of Africa's conflicts fit this new paradigm. The old steady the military coup is still a common form of political upheaval, as Guinea found out in 2008 and Madagascar not too long thereafter. But though their political grievances are well defined, the organizations they "lead" are not. Old-style African rebels spent years in the bush honing their leadership skills, polishing their ideology, and learning to deliver services before they ever met a Western diplomat or sat for a television interview. Now rebels are hoisted out of obscurity after they have little more than a website and a "press office" The sad fact is that draw for many of these rebel "leaders" was not the negotiating sessions, but the all-you-can-eat buffet and a couple of nights in a five-star hotel. This is what many conflicts in Africa have become circles of violence in the bush, with no end in sight.

Hollywood star George Clooney has launched an initiative aimed at ending conflicts in Africa by tracking the money that fuels them. The Sentry, founded by Clooney and John Prendergast of an advocacy group called the Enough Project, will probe the financing of conflicts in South Sudan, Sudan, Central African Republic and Democratic Republic of Congo.

"Real leverage for peace and human rights will come when the people who benefit from war will pay a price for the damage they cause," the 54-year old Oscar-winner, who has a long history as an advocate for peace in Sudan and South Sudan, said in a statement. "conventional tools of diplomacy" had so far failed and "new efforts must centre on how to make war costlier than peace". "The objective of The Sentry is to follow the money and deny those war profiteers the proceeds from their crimes," said Prendergast.

In 2010, Clooney and Prendergast initiated the Satellite Sentinel Project, using satellites to map evidence of conflict and human rights abuses on the ground. At that time, the fear was of war between Khartoum and Juba as the south prepared for its independence in July 2011. But in late 2013, civil war broke out inside the new nation of South Sudan and the satellite project was left largely redundant. The Sentry's declared goal is to "dismantle the networks of perpetrators, facilitators and enablers who fund and profit from Africa's deadliest conflicts." Participants in the project include C4ADS, a Washington-based non-profit research organisation, and activist group Not On Our Watch, co-founded by Hollywood actors Clooney, Don Cheadle, Matt Damon and Brad Pitt.

The Sentry's first briefing paper on South Sudan was damning. It described the civil war between President Salva Kiir and his former deputy Riek Machar as "a competition among the nation's elite for power and profits," with warring parties fighting for control of "a kleptocratic regime that has captured and controlled nearly all profit-generating sectors of the economy". The group hopes a focus on "economic enablers" identifying the banks, businessmen, investors and corrupt officials who launder gains and connect corrupt politicians and militiamen to financial markets will provide new pressure to end long-running conflicts in Africa. "To effectively address the conflict in South Sudan requires looking beyond the spasms of horrific violence and focusing on the underlying drivers, namely the various trends that collectively constitute South Sudan's violent kleptocratic system," The Sentry said.

The rich mineral mines of the Democratic Republic of Congo supply valuable minerals to the tech industry, but they come at a deadly cost that is finally being faced. The money that helped prolong the suffering of war in the Congo flowed from the likes of you, me, and just about anyone else who bought a PC, phone, or electronic gadget in recent memory. Inside many of these electronic devices are components that began life as minerals dug at gunpoint from mines in the DRC. The misery that of war in DRC because of their mineral wealth has brought to the DRC people to their knees. The Congolese population is forced to dig for the mineral cassiterite and panning for gold in a nearby river which will be enjoyed in the West and East. Facts are that slavery is still being practised in the Congo with Child labour prevailing in most of the mines. "Sometimes people worked 24 hours out of 24, night and day, using head-mounted lamps one team working days and one doing nights. At the time there were no rules, and sometimes miners died of fatigue. There were also deaths because the pits were deep and there was flooding," Their suffering has been at the hands of Hutu and Tutsi fighters, and corrupt officers within the Congolese army, who have seen the mines as a way of funding the armed conflict that has raged sporadically in the country since 1998.

The minerals from the DRC's mines have changed hands innumerable times on their journey to our PCs and phones. After being dug up in central Africa the minerals travel through a long and snaking chain of suppliers, travelling to Asia and elsewhere to be smelted into metals and then onto the wider world where they end up in electronics, as well in vehicles and jewellery. The complexity and length of that supply chain is such that for years electronics firms claimed it was opaque, that determining whether their products were perpetuating a cycle of killings and rape in the DRC was an insurmountable task, both financially and logistically. Today attitudes are changing as companies prepare to face up to the requirements of new legislation requiring them to track these minerals right back to the mine they were dug. Companies registered with the US Securities and Exchange Commission (SEC) will have to disclose the use of conflict minerals sourced from the DRC or its neighbouring countries in their products under section 1502 of the U.S. Dodd-Frank Wall Street Reform and Consumer Protection Act (PDF). Companies must file their first reports with the SEC by the end of May 2014.

Inside many of these electronic devices are components that began life as minerals dug at gunpoint from mines in the DRC. If firms find that the minerals do originate from the DRC or an adjoining country, they are required to report on their efforts to determine the mine or location of origin to ensure that armed groups are not benefiting from the trade of these minerals.

By shining a spotlight on electronics manufacturers' supply chains, legislators are hoping to pressure companies to invest in removing conflict minerals from their products. But while major US-registered electronics firms are outwardly pledging to end the use of conflict minerals some of these same firms belong to industry associations that are seeking to water down the disclosure requirements under Dodd-Frank. The U.S. Chamber of Commerce, the Business Roundtable, and the National Association of Manufacturers have mounted a legal challenge to the obligations, which is being considered by the U.S. Court of Appeals. The group is seeking to overturn the disclosure requirement, and have it rewritten in a less strict form. They argue that it imposes too many costs, goes beyond congressional intent, and violates First Amendment freedoms by forcing companies to condemn their own products. The challenge won some sympathy with one of the judges at a hearing in January 2014, who raised the prospect of the requirement creating a "slippery slope problem" in relation to US companies having to disclose the conditions under which their products are manufactured overseas. The judges have yet to indicate when they will make a ruling on the challenge. Some electronics manufacturers, such as Microsoft and Motorola, have distanced themselves from this legal challenge.

The European Commission is also considering implementing a voluntary scheme under which European Union (EU)-registered smelters selling materials derived from minerals from the DRC and other conflict zones worldwide could be certified as conflict-free. The proposal has been attacked as "weak," and a disappointment to campaigners who found most EU companies not required to comply with Dodd-Frank have done minimal work to remove conflict minerals from their supply chain. The three main conflict minerals are cassiterite, Coltan, and wolframite, sometimes referred to under the acronym 3T, a reference to the tin, tantalum, and tungsten metals derived from them. The fourth conflict material is gold.

The majority of US-registered computer component and PC manufacturers are currently attempting to document their supply chains and remove conflict minerals via the Conflict-Free Smelter Program (CFSP). The programme is run by the Electronic Industry Citizenship Coalition, an electronics industry body that works to make supply chains more socially, environmentally, and economically friendly, and the Global e-Sustainability Initiative (GeSI).

Major electronics firms among the more than 120 companies participating in the CFSP include are AMD; Apple; Dell; HP; Intel; Microsoft and Nokia. Many of the large electronics firms are also engaged in their own private efforts to clean up their supply chains. Although progress varies, Intel made headlines when it pledged that no conflict minerals will be used to manufacture its microprocessors as of January 2014. The company travelled more than 250,000 miles to visit more than 80 smelters in 21 countries to verify its microprocessor supply chain is conflict free and is working with partners in the CFSP. Under the CFSP, which is part of the wider Conflict-Free Sourcing Initiative (CFSI), a whitelist is being built of smelters and refiners that don't use conflict minerals, as determined by third-party auditors.

To date more than 70 smelters have been listed as conflict-free under the CFSP, providing computer makers with a source of metals that isn't perpetuating abuses by armed groups in central Africa. Smelters are assessed against the OECD Due Diligence Guidelines for Responsible Supply Chains of Minerals (PDF), which provides recommendations for how companies can respect human rights and avoid contributing to conflict when sourcing minerals. The CFSI has validated smelters for all four metals derived from conflict minerals tantalum, tin, tungsten, and gold as being conflict-free. Unsurprisingly, the CFSI and schemes is run by jewellery and gold bullions trade groups has limitations, which means it isn't a silver bullet when it comes to severing the decades old link between the western consumer goods and the central African mines where abuses are perpetrated.

At present there simply aren't enough of these conflict-free smelters to meet the needs of the world's biggest computer makers. Even HP, the world's largest server maker, and a firm that was rated as having made the second most progress of any electronics manufacturer in the world by the Enough Project in 2012, said that of the just over 200 smelters it deals with only about 60 are certified as conflict-free. And of these 60 conflict-free smelters, only four or five source minerals from inside the DRC.

Apple revealed similar figures earlier in 2014. It has verified 59 smelters in its supply chain as conflict-free, but 104 of its smelters use minerals whose origins are unknown. Boycotting one of the world's poorest countries, because of the lack of mines within the DRC certified as being conflict-free, some smelters have stopped sourcing minerals from the DRC and its adjoining countries in order to gain a conflict-free status. This de facto boycott limits the DRC's ability to sell its trillions of dollars' worth of untapped mineral wealth, in a country ranked by the UN as one of the poorest in the world, with the average annual income per person just $286 in 2012.

"The biggest loophole in our view is that many companies are moving to withdraw from the DRC and that is not what we want to see companies doing. What we would like to see companies doing is to stay in the region and try to do their best to influence it in a positive way," said Gisela ten Kate who wrote a report into the use of conflict minerals by European companies for the pressure group SOMO. Since the pull out of the electronics companies there has been a tremendous surge by the Congolese government and local mining companies seeking an alternative market with the Chinese. The price these Chinese smelters are willing to pay for minerals varies but is generally far lower than what miners were previously receiving. In the case of the tin ore cassiterite, it's roughly one third of what miners were receiving previously, he said. In 2013 tantalum ore Coltan from the North Kivu region was reported to be selling for one tenth the price it fetched in the early 2000s.

Cleaning up mining operations in the DRC so they no longer fund militias, don't use child labour, and introduce safer working conditions is a massive undertaking. There are around 5,000 mines in the North and South Kivu region of Eastern Congo. These mines employed tens of thousands of people at their peak, although the de facto embargo has reduced the scale of mining operations in the region, with trade in tin almost collapsing in North Kivu according to a November 2013 report from the region. In these mines, adults and children dug minerals with very basic tools or their hands, without safety training or equipment, and in mines under militia control forced labour was not uncommon. Fatalities and serious accidents were a regular occurrence, and still are in operating mines.

While on paper South African and Canadian firms hold the exploration rights to many of the mines in Eastern Congo, the violence in the region led many of them to pull out, which resulted in groups of what are called artisanal miners moving in. Artisanal miners are small groups who illegally work the mining concessions in the region. These are the miners that have historically fallen under the control of armed groups, who extracted money from them through taxes and extortion. Today there is an opportunity to reform the way the mines are run, as unlike much of the past 15 years, the majority of 3T mines in Eastern Congo are free of armed groups. Most significantly, this includes the Bisie mine in North Kivu that accounted for about 70% of cassiterite coming out of the region. Nevertheless, militias remain in control of some mines.

And while 3T mines are largely outside of militia control, the same can't be said for the gold mines, which are still largely run by armed groups, both militias, and the Congolese army. The difference stems from the ease with which gold can be smuggled over the border and sold as if originating from a different country. Even small quantities of gold, which can be transported and hidden with relative ease, can fetch a high price over the border, he said. By comparison, the tonnes of 3T minerals that would need to be sneaked out of the DRC to make the risk financially worthwhile make smuggling difficult.

But even with the armed groups no longer controlling the majority of the 3T mines, reforming how thousands of mines are run in a country just under one quarter the size of the US is going to take time, "Asking people to change the way they do business is not easy," "But if they realise if they do not conform to what is required, they are not going to sell." The country has very few roads or railways to speak of, and instability, corruption, and a lack of infrastructure have slowed the rate at which mines inside the country can be certified as having safe working conditions and being outside of militia control, said Jay Celorie, global program manager for conflict minerals at HP. "It's a result of those other things that really should be provided by the government that aren't available, as opposed to the private sector not wanting to mine those areas," he said. "In order to have traceability somebody has to pay for that cost of traceability and so you need a mining company that's willing to make that investment and ensure that happens."

The capacity of the Congolese state to oversee the artisanal mining sector is also extremely limited. Along with corruption, their ability to oversee the territory under their responsibility is also held back by a lack of means, personnel, resources, and technical knowledge. Reforming conditions in mines in the North Kivu region, which has the largest tin and other mineral deposits, had proved impossible until recently because an armed group named M23 was active in the region. But the defeat of M23 in November 2013, when the group signed a peace treaty with the Congolese government, has spurred some affiliated militias to lay down their weapons, and electronics firms are beginning to show interest in helping to set up new mining operations.

"US electronics companies Intel, Motorola, HP, and others they have come to the ground and are thinking now of launching pilot projects at a number of mines in Masisi a province in North Kivu, which is good news," "This would not be possible if the M23 was still active." The defeat of M23 was in part attributed to the efforts of the UN intervention brigade, a complement of UN soldiers working with the Congolese army to suppress the armed groups in Eastern DRC. Art isanal miners in North and South Kivu regions have been organising into co-operatives. These co-operatives allow mines to be registered as meeting certain standards and issued with mining permits.

"There have also been a lot of campaigns sensitising people about the working conditions in mines, the fact that OECD due diligence requires no use of children, no exploitation of women sexually, the banning of illegal taxes, that only the mining police should be securing the mine and the trading routes. So, all of these are being put together," Trading centres or "centre de négoce" for minerals have also been constructed that aims to ensure no illegal taxes will be levied along trading routes. These centres also monitor the level of militarisation at sites supplying them with minerals and provide a site where miners can sell minerals for guaranteed prices, set to their value on the London Stock Exchange.

Work is taking place to finalise a regulatory framework to certify the conditions in which minerals are being mined in the DRC and the neighbouring country of Rwanda. The framework for mineral certification, known as the International Conference on the Great Lakes Region (ICGLR) Regional Initiative against the Exploitation of Natural Resources, will put in place measures for third-party inspections, audits of mines, and combating fraud and mineral smuggling, as well as setting up a database for mineral tracking.

One such programme is the German Federal Institute for Geosciences and Natural Resources' (BGR) Certified Trading Chains scheme, which aims to demonstrate minerals have been produced in a responsible way and to develop ethical trading chains. The BGR is also setting up a fingerprint analysis database system in Eastern DRC that will analyse minerals for a chemical signature linked to a particular mine, allowing the provenance of those minerals to be checked.

The tin industry association, International Tin Research Institute (ITRI), has developed a traceability system (iTSCi) that is used to monitor the origins of 3T minerals in the DRC. Under the iTSCi scheme 3T minerals are bagged and tagged with the mine they were dug from, so they can be traced through the supply chain from the mine to the finished product. Mines are visited by representatives of the UN, the BGR, the Congolese government, civil society, and local mining companies to certify they are free of armed groups and respecting human rights. iTSCi is also being extended into the previously conflict-stricken North Kivu province for the first time, with the scheme being set up in mines in Rubaya, west of Goma. According to the Enough Project, by February 2013 a total of 20 mining sites had been validated as conflict free in North and South Kivu. "It is still at an early stage simply because most of the mines are in very remote areas, and since we still have rogue armed groups here and there, you never know. But also, more significantly, the fact that Congo is lacking communications infrastructure in terms of roads, so we need to go step by step,"

Who supplies Arms to Africa? In September 2014 South African authorities seized $9.3 million stashed in three suitcases on a private Nigerian jet, sparking a fallout between the two countries, which have in recent years maintained an uneasy relationship. Nigerian authorities said the cash, all in $100 bills, was meant for legitimate arms purchases, as it sought to turn the tide following criticism over its fumbled handling of the Boko Haram insurgency. The militants have been active since 2009, but it is only in recent weeks that a regional multinational force has gained an undisputed battlefield advantage over the group, which is blamed for nearly 15,000 deaths mainly in north-eastern Nigeria. Those gains are not by chance Nigeria and Cameroon have in recent months been recipients of several arms deliveries, new data on international arms transfers from the Stockholm International Peace Research Institute (SIPRI) shows.

In an interview President Goodluck Jonathan blamed the military's inability to put down the rebellion previously to a lack of weapons and resources, which have now come through. It is in keeping with global trends showing an upward swing in arms exports, with the volumes in 2010-2014 some 16% higher than in the preceding five years. The US, Russia, China, Germany and France are the five biggest exporters, while India, Saudi Arabia, China, the UAE and Pakistan took most deliveries globally.

I looked at the arms transfer sales data on Africa, ahead of the release of military expenditure figures by the Sweden-based research institution.

1: Africa received 9% of all global arms deliveries between 2010-14, the least of all the regions, but still a 45% increase over 2005-2009. SIPRI uses a five-year moving average due to yearly fluctuations in arms sales numbers.

2: States in sub-Saharan Africa received 42% of all imports into the continent, led by rivals Sudan and Uganda as the largest importers, at 15% and 14% of the subregional total respectively. Sudan is battling rebels internally, while Uganda has in recent years assumed the role of regional policeman, seen in intervention in countries such as South Sudan, DR Congo (with disastrous consequences), Central African Republic, and its on-going participation in peacekeeping operations such as in Somalia.

3: Despite these figures, understanding the impact of arms sales to Africa can be a bit like groping in the dark. In many cases they fuel conflict, in others they are used legitimately for defence or peacekeeping operations. These grey areas are why it is so difficult to get accurate data on the continent while countries in the region regularly express support for conventional arms control initiatives, their low level of participation in the UN Register of Conventional Arms (UNROCA) the key intergovernmental reporting instrument on conventional arms casts doubts on their willingness to actively control arms. Just seven African countries have ratified the Arms Trade Treaty which came into force in December for example.

4: With China, the US and Russia among the biggest suppliers to Africa, their motives are diverse from direct financial gain to "strengthening political influence in sub-Saharan Africa in order to gain access to natural resources and to further the security interest of the supplier," SIPRI notes in a policy paper on the region. The outcome is a different interpretation of rules such as UN embargoes, more often not contributing to conflict in the region.

5: The three largest importers in the continent 2010-14 were Algeria which is in conflict with rebel groups and which took 30% of imports into the region, Morocco (26%) and Sudan, which took stock of 6% of arms.

6: The US restarted deliveries to Egypt in 2014, which it had restrained following the military coup in the country in 2013. SIPRI says the most notable delivery was for 10 combat helicopters, considered key in Egypt's military campaign against Sinai rebels.

7: Neighbours Morocco and Algeria appear to be involved in an arms race of sorts the latter increased deliveries by 3% between 2005-09 and 2010-14, buying its stock from Italy, Russia and China. Morocco saw imports increased elevenfold over the same period. Algiers appears to have the last laugh it has a raft of outstanding orders, unlike its rival.

8: Several suppliers sent weapons to Nigeria and Cameroon to fulfil their urgent need for equipment to fight militant group Boko Haram, widely blamed for the terrorists' longevity, despite the former spending twice as much on defence as on education. Both countries last year ordered and received choppers from China and Russia, and armoured vehicles from China, South Africa, Ukraine and Czech Republic.

9: African independent companies have also taken advantage of the war against the Islamic State. Ivor Ichikowitz, the founder of Africa's biggest privately-owned arms company Paramount Group, recently won an order to sell 50 armoured vehicles worth more than $1 million each to Jordan. He expects more business to follow with Middle Eastern governments looking to bolster their defences.

10: Despite this, no African company features among SIPRI's list (pdf) of the world's 100 largest arms-producing and military services companies, which in 2013 saw combined sales of $402 billion or a fifth of Africa's GDP. Two thirds of the firms are headquartered either in the US or Western Europe. The last entry on the list made $770 million in sales in that year.

A graphical representation of the presence of American and French troops in Africa. The West has in recent years renewed its enthusiasm for African military expeditions. A graphical representation of the presence of American and French troops in Africa. The West has in recent years renewed its enthusiasm for African military expeditions.

The willingness to send troops into Africa has seen long-rested western powers stir into action, including Germany. The German plan was a result of lobbying by France for the European Union to send troops into CAR. Paris has seen its historical role in Africa bloom again, and is seeing even the United States, chastened after its December 1992 to March 1994 Somalia "Operation Restore Hope" debacle, tentatively put out feelers on the continent. The West is having to tread carefully, given echoes of its past on the continent but this has not dampened the growing military enthusiasm to intervene widely.

More than any colonial power, the French hardly foresaw or accepted decolonisation, having attached not only tremendous material but also symbolic value to its colonies. Therefore, even after independence, France continued to extract benefits from its former colonies through secret agreements. In order to continue to exact leverage over most of its former African colonies, France signed a host of secretive agreements heavily weighted in its favour. The agreements, which were part of the Colonial Pact, gave France an upper hand over these countries' resources, as well as their military affairs. Part of the agreement gave France the legal right to intervene militarily in African countries, and also to station troops permanently in bases and military facilities exclusively run by the French.

The pact also forbade these countries from seeking other military alliances except the one Paris had offered them. This made most of the Francophone countries France's pré carré (private preserve) even after independence. Between 1962-1995, France intervened militarily in African countries 19 times. During the last 50 years, a total of 67 coups happened in 26 countries in Africa; 16 of those countries are French ex-colonies. But their series of blunders during the Rwandan genocide, the 1996-1997 and the Zaire crisis in which they continued to support the collapsing government of Mobutu Sese Seko—combined with tough economic realities at home saw France reset its Africa engagement, dropping its unilateral approach in favour of multilateral cooperation. The military coup in Mali in 2012 and the current Central Africa crisis has seen France increase its military footprint and activities in Africa once again. At the request of the Malian government, on January 11, 2013 France launched military operations against insurgent targets in northern. This brought back the memories of previous French interventions.

In the ongoing crisis in Central African Republic, France has also taken a prominent role. Overall, according to the French Ministry of Defence, in February 2013, of 10,025 military personnel deployed overseas, 4,610 were in West Africa, 2,180 in Central Africa and 270 were involved in anti-piracy operations in the Gulf of Aden.

The United States, during the Cold War, US foreign policy was fairly clear, it was based on "US vs. Them", "them" being the Communists and their allies. The central strategy was containment of the Communist. After the end of the Cold War, buoyed by the defeat of the USSR, US foreign policy embarked on "The New World Order". The US saw and acted as the uncontested leader of this new order. Multilateralism rather than unilateralism was now the byword.

Saddam Hussein was the first to face the wrath of multilateralism when in 1990 he invaded Kuwait. Then US president George H. Bush cobbled together a coalition of 34 countries; a force numbering between 500,000–600,000 with the blessing of the United Nations. Saddam was defeated. Shortly after, the US embarked on another foreign expedition, this time in Somalia to contain the warlords ravaging the country. This proved more difficult than anticipated. The humanitarian effort dubbed Operation Restore Hope that was launched with fanfare quickly turned sour, when some 18 US servicemen were killed.

After being chastised over the Somalia operation, the US remains famously reticent to committing troops in intractable "tribal" conflicts in far flung areas. The bombing of the US embassies in Nairobi and Dar es Salaam in 1998 brought home the reality of transnational non-state actors. Their engagement shifted the nature of the war, the strategy and the operation.

The safety and security of US personnel, safeguarding of critical trade routes, combined with the emergence of China, has seen the US increase its resources and operations in Africa. The United States Africa Command (AFRICOM), established in 2007, is the main vehicle of Washington's new security-focused policy towards Africa. The Horn of Africa and Sahel are the two regions the US has increasingly focused on in its counter- terrorism efforts.

In the Horn, the Combined Joint Task Force-Horn of Africa (CJTF- HOA), established in 2001, and based at Camp Lemonnier, Djibouti, is the American military's main operational presence in Horn of Africa, where it has an estimated 4,000 troops. The key role here is to destabilise and destroy Al Shabaab the Somali-based Islamist group linked to Al Qaeda.

In Somalia, the US has deployed about two dozen regular troops to advise the fragile government of Hassan Shekh Mahmoud. Following the breakout of conflict in South Sudan early this year, the US deployed 45 military personnel to protect its citizens and their property. After Camp Lemonnier, the largest US deployment is in Entebbe in Uganda. A total of 300 military officers are stationed in a dilapidated compound that has recently received a huge facelift. Their key function here is to look for Lord's Resistance Army leader Joseph Kony. In Camp Simba, located in the remote Manda Bay in Lamu, Kenya, there are an estimated 60 military officers stationed there since the end of 2013.

In West Africa according to the White House, there are about 100 US military personnel in Niamey Niger. Following Boko Haram's abduction of the school children, the US sent 70 military personnel in Nigeria, with 50 regularly assigned to the US Embassy, and 20 Marines there for training. The US has announced it was sending 80 troops to Chad as part of the team to help in rescuing the Nigerian school children abducted by Boko Haram. There are a number of US military personnel in Ethiopia, Burkina Faso, Central African Republic, Congo and Mali, but it is difficult to establish their numbers. The known total number of US troops in Africa is 4,680, combined with the classified ones; the actual number could conservatively be anywhere between 4,000- 6,000.

The British army also has a Training Unit in Kenya, BATUK, which provides logistic support to visiting units. There are around 56 permanent staff and reinforcing short tour cohort of another 110 personnel, according to its data. Sudan was awash with arms long before the country split in two. When South Sudan seceded in 2011, it was estimated that there were up to 3.2m small arms in circulation. Two-thirds of these were thought to be in the hands of civilians. Since then, arms have proliferated on both sides of the recently devised border with fatal results. In Sudan, a country often dubbed "Africa's arms dump", the number of arms is rising by the day amid armed conflict between government forces, paramilitaries, rebels, hired militia, foreign fighters, bandits as well as inter- and intra-communal warfare. This aggression is fuelled by the global arms trade and smuggling from neighbouring states.

A similar story is heard in South Sudan, where ownership of guns and small arms is estimated to have sharply increased during its three years as an independent nation, partly due to the number of rebel and militia groups that sprung up in Jonglei and Upper Nile states in 2010 and 2011. Arms are a common sight and ammunition can be bought for around US$1 per cartridge at some local markets. The arrival of firearms, Illegal gun ownership in both countries can be traced back to major historical events. Guns arrived with the invading armies of Muhammad Ali Pasha in the early 19th century. Firearms were also introduced by the British-led Anglo-Egyptian Condominium forces during the reconquest of Sudan in 1898. It wasn't until the 1950s that civilians started to own firearms in significant numbers, research shows, partly because of the 1955 mutiny which sowed the seeds of the first southern rebellion.

During these years, southern Sudanese soldiers raided military bases, stole weapons and fled into the forest, just one of the ways that light weapons found their way north into the hands of various groups located on what would later become the border. Meanwhile, research has shown the international role in weapon supply, with former West Germany introducing automatic small arms in vast numbers to Sudan, which, until then, mainly had old British carbines. West Germany also set up the ammunition factory in Sheggera, Khartoum, in effect, providing the bullets to keep the guns firing. In the 1980s, East Germany responded by supplying the Sudan People's Liberation Army (SPLA) with AK47s via Ethiopia. In this way, Cold War animosities were played out in the Greater Horn of Africa.

Historians say liberation movements, especially those in neighbouring countries, fanned the spread of firearms in Sudan and the trade in illegal weapons. A rare evidence of how politically motivated arms deals spiralled out of control as guns proliferated followed the assassination of Congolese independence leader Patrice Lumumba. The first transitional government after the 1964 October revolution in Khartoum supplied West German G3 assault rifles to the Simba rebels. When they were defeated in 1965, the Southern Sudanese separatist rebel group Anyanya acquired many of those German guns.

Then, in 1976, forces associated with Sudanese opposition figures attacked districts in Khartoum in an attempt to seize power from President Jaafar Mohammed Al Nimeiri, troops which had been trained and equipped in Libya. Within three days the attackers were driven back, but they left a lasting legacy: thousands of small arms and other weapons made their way to civilians in western Sudan. Historical records show that arms proliferation in Darfur, meanwhile, dates from the 1960s.

In a published working paper, Sudanese researcher and retired Major Abdel Karim Abdel Farraj highlighted other ways guns spread in Sudan. Conflicts, including the Libya-Chad war of the 1980s, "contributed to the influx of small arms and light weaponry into Sudan, and in particular Darfur, which, due to the region's vast size and the lack of control of both central and local authorities, received weaponry that outmatched the arsenal of both the police and armed forces."

According to Abdel Karim Abdel, the decades-long southern war was the primary source of the weapons inundation, especially after 1983, when the late Libyan leader Colonel Muammar Gaddafi supported the opposition forces, stoked by his personal animosity towards Jaafar Al Nimeiri. The arming of proxy tribal militias was the handiwork of elected governments in Khartoum in 1986-89, who provided weapons for the Baggara to fight against the SPLA.

The Libya-Chad war of the 1980s "contributed to the influx of small arms and light weaponry into Sudan, and in particular Darfur, which received weaponry that outmatched the arsenal of both the police and armed forces. The organisation Saferworld says arms were distributed among citizens by the Khartoum government or the Sudan Peoples' Liberation Army (SPLA) in the years before the signing of the comprehensive peace agreement.

"In Lakes State in today's South Sudan, the SPLA provided weapons to cattle keepers to enable them to protect themselves and their communities from cattle raiders. The arming of these youth groups, known as the gelweng, allowed the SPLA to shift their focus and efforts from community security to the ongoing war with the north," Saferworld wrote in a report.

"And even after the government signed the peace treaty with the rebels in 2005, ending the decades of civil war, civilians including the gelweng in Lakes State kept hold of their weapons, in case they needed to defend themselves. Apart from government provision of small arms to non-state actors, weapons have also reached civilians through porous borders with neighbouring countries. According to the report Following the Thread: Arms and Ammunition Tracing in Sudan and South Sudan, released in May 2014 by the Swiss research group Small Arms Survey, these weapons spread "either for the intentional purpose of selling or trading, or because armed nomadic groups travel throughout the border regions with their weapons".

A South Sudanese example of this is the Kidepo valley that straddles South Sudan, Uganda and Kenya. For many years valley residents, the Turkana of Kenya, the Dodoth of Uganda and the Toposa of South Sudan, have traded arms across the three countries' borders. The three groups share ethnic and linguistic roots and are all pastoralists. Given a constant threat of cattle raiding among these communities, they often traffic small arms, acquiring guns to protect their livestock or raid each other.

Arms continue to move across the Sudan's mutual border to this very day. It is believed that communities in South Sudan's northern states of Northern Bahr el Ghazal, Warrap and Upper Nile procure small arms from Sudan. Sudanese traders or nomads are thought to supply small arms and ammunition, but in limited quantities to individual buyers. Tribal groups and rebel militias seeking larger amounts of arms and ammunition have to import from neighbouring countries. Tribal militias like the South Sudanese White Army (Nuer Youth from Jonglei and Upper Nile states) procure weapons and ammunition locally from traders across the border from Ethiopia's Gambella region, according to Jonah Leff, Director of Operations at Conflict Armament Research, which maps arms flows in conflict zones.

Most small arms that are available from traders locally are AK-type assault rifles. PKM machine guns and RPGs are also available, but in much smaller quantities. However, German HK G3 rifles sometimes cross the border from Ethiopia and Kenya, "In the local market rifles cost between US$150- 250 depending on the condition and make but people often purchase rifles with cattle. It has been said in the state of Jonglei, "if the gun is new you pay one heifer and an ox. If it's old, you may pay only a cow."

But the origin of many firearms remains murky. In Sudan, the Khartoum government and opposition rebel movements frequently trade accusations over who is responsible for the spread of arms within the country. In December 2013, Interior Minister Ibrahim Mahmoud described: "the widespread availability of weapons among Sudan's tribes, especially in the districts of Darfur," adding, that rebel movements were the reason for their availability in tribal circles."

In a report submitted to the Council of States, Sudan's upper house of parliament, entitled "All the Tribes Are Now Armed", the minister said: "tribes operate on the principle that there can be no security except through the possession of weapons." Due to lack of security, but rebel movements met the minister's claims with an accusation of their own. "Responsibility for the spread of weapons and militarisation of the country's tribes lies solely at the feet of the Khartoum regime, in its efforts to retain power and to obtain and preserve wealth," said Adam Salih, military spokesman of the Sudanese Liberation Movement's Minnawi faction. "The Revolutionary Front has a hand in the matter."

"South Sudan has not systematically destroyed surplus or non-serviceable firearms since obtaining independence in 2011," the report said, adding that the government failed to record its arms stockpiles, meaning the weapons can be taken illicitly. A mixture of poor training and poor pay means that organised forces of South Sudan including military, police, prison services, wildlife wardens, and the fire brigade have been reported to pass on weapons to the civilian population. Soldiers meanwhile, have been accused of reselling collected weapons to the population after they were removed during disarmament campaigns. Years of animosity between Sudan and South Sudan sped up the flow of arms in both countries. Researchers suggested that in the last few years the Sudanese government may have supplied small arms and ammunition to some of the rebels and militia groups fighting to topple the government in Juba and provided weapons and ammunition to David Yau Yau's rebels in December 2012.

The weapons, which some indicate may have been delivered by airdrops, including a type of Chinese rifle that had never before been observed in South Sudan called the CQ, which is a copy of an M16. The second rifle was an A30 RPG-type rocket launcher that was being manufactured by the Yarmouk factory in Sudan.

Sudan, meanwhile, said it has clear evidence of South Sudan supporting rebels beyond their national border, including providing weapons. South Sudan repeatedly challenged the allegations which President Salva Kiir, at the time, dubbed as tantamount to an indirect declaration of war. Whoever has a gun in his hand protects his life: this belief which prevails in many regions in Sudan and South Sudan and the spiralling civilian ownership of firearms poses a serious threat to life.

Armed robbery and pillage are widespread in both countries, facilitated by the availability of weapons. These crimes are mainly carried out by "highwaymen" who position themselves along roads day and night, threatening pedestrians and vehicles, stealing possessions and money before fleeing. These robberies frequently result in bloodshed, particularly when victims seek to resist with weapons of their own. Previously, such crimes were only found in Sudan's distant regions, far from any effective state control, but in recent times they have started to take place inside major cities.

In its report, Saferworld paints a similar portrait of everyday violence in South Sudan: "One only needs to read the newspaper on any given day to understand the problem that the proliferation of small arms has caused in South Sudan. For instance, armed robberies in urban centres, the hijacking of vehicles, aid vehicles being detained, hundreds killed in cattle raiding, hundreds more killed in revenge attacks such incidents are devastatingly common throughout South Sudan."

Meanwhile, the inability of governments in Juba and Khartoum to provide security within their respective countries feeds internal demand for arms. South Sudanese people feel the pressing need to protect themselves since the outbreak of violence in December 2013 and the spread of fighting to Jonglei, Upper Nile and Unity states. Until South Sudan can provide safe home for its citizens, "arms will remain a household feature," said Leff, from Conflict Armament Research.

Meanwhile, in Sudan, many sectors of society view arms as a necessity, despite harsh punishments for bearing arms and for importing weapons without a license. Carrying weapons is especially important among pastoralists along the borders of West Sudan in Darfur, through greater Kordofan and the Nuba Mountains, Blue Nile and into eastern Sudan.

A mix of ongoing fear and established patterns of behaviour has made citizens across Sudan and South Sudan loathe to give up weapons. This gives rise to a tragic vicious circle whereby surging gun ownership boosts insecurity which, in turn, persuades more people they need a gun. It is only by tackling these root causes that Sudan and South Sudan can hope to free the region from the scourge of arms. The arms flow started way, way back before "the West" (and Israel) decided to take a side in the Sudan conflict. It's clearly stated that Gaddafi himself was responsible for the sudden boom in weapons proliferation starting in the 1980s.

U.S. Arms to Africa and the Congo War by William D. Hartung and Bridget Moix of the Arms Trade Resource Center "We hope to build a new and lasting partnership between Africa and the world, based on common interests, mutual respect, and a shared commitment to peace, prosperity, and freedom." The U.S. Secretary of State Madeleine Albright Statement to the UN Security Council Ministerial on Africa, Sept. 24, 1998

"When the United States assumes the Presidency of the Security Council next month, in January 2000 the first month of the first year of the new millennium I wish to announce today that we intend to make Africa the priority of the month." U.S. Permanent Representative to the United Nations Richard Holbrooke Pretoria, South Africa, Dec. 6, 1999

"The problem of all the ethnic and tribal wars must be either resolved or at least largely reduced through a big effort by the countries that deal in arms to prevent the over-militarisation of Africa."- Managing Director of the International Monetary Fund Michel Camdessus Comments to French radio, Jan. 2, 2000

As the Clinton administration moves into the presidency of the United Nations Security Council, it is declaring January 2000, "the month of Africa." Hoping to counter criticisms that it has been engaged in a rhetorical promotion of U.S.-Africa relations over the past two years without substantive follow-up, the administration has announced its intent to prioritize finding solutions to the ongoing conflicts in the region, including a 30-year civil war that trudges on in Angola and the ongoing crisis in the Democratic Republic of the Congo (DRC). It has not, however, accepted its own responsibility in helping to create the conditions that have led to these seemingly intractable conflicts.

Over the past few years, the administration has made considerable effort to put a new and improved face on its relations with African countries. High-level visits to the region first by Secretary of State Madeleine Albright, then President Clinton himself in the spring of 1998, and U.S. Ambassador to the UN Richard Holbrooke have reinforced the idea of a new partnership with the continent based on promoting "African solutions to African problems." The reality, however, is that the problems facing Africa and her people are violent conflict, political instability, and the lowest regional rate of economic growth worldwide have been fuelled in part by a legacy of U.S. involvement in the region. Moreover, the solutions being proposed by the Clinton administration remain grounded in the counter-productive Cold-War policies that have defined U.S.-Africa relations for far too long.

Unfortunately, the ongoing war in the Democratic Republic of the Congo presents a vivid example of how U.S. policies past and present have failed the people of Africa. After more than two years of devastating war, African leaders are struggling, with little success, to implement the Lusaka peace accord. Signatories to the treaty continue to call for UN peacekeeping support even as they prepare for continued fighting. Despite its demonstrable role in planting the seeds of this conflict, the U.S. has done little to either acknowledge its complicity or help create a viable resolution. Official tours of the region and impressive rhetoric will not be enough to contribute to lasting peace, democratic stability, and economic development in Africa.

Due to the continuing legacies of its Cold War policies toward Africa, the U.S. bears some responsibility for the cycles of violence and economic problems plaguing the continent. Throughout the Cold War (1950-1989), the U.S. delivered over $1.5 billion worth of weaponry to Africa. Many of the top U.S. arms clients Liberia, Somalia, the Sudan, and DRC have turned out to be the top basket cases of the 1990s in terms of violence, instability, and economic collapse. The ongoing civil war in the Democratic Republic of the Congo (formerly Zaire) is a prime example of the devastating legacy of U.S. arms sales policy on Africa. The U.S. prolonged the rule of Zairian dictator Mobutu Sese Soko by providing more than $300 million in weapons and $100 million in military training. Mobutu used his U.S. supplied arsenal to repress his own people and plunder his nation's economy for three decades, until his brutal regime was overthrown by Laurent Kabila's forces in 1997.

When Kabila took power, the Clinton administration quickly offered military support by developing a plan for new training operations with the armed forces. Although the Clinton administration has been quick to criticize the governments involved in the Congo War, decades of U.S. weapons transfers and continued military training to both sides of the conflict have helped fuel the fighting.

The U.S. has helped build the arsenals of eight of the nine governments directly involved in the war that has ravaged the DRC since Kabila's coup. U.S. military transfers in the form of direct government-to-government weapons deliveries, commercial sales, and International Military Education and Training (IMET) to the states directly involved have totalled more than $125 million since the end of the Cold War. Despite the failure of U.S. polices in the region, the current administration continues to respond to Africa's woes by helping to strengthen African militaries. As U.S. weapons deliveries to Africa continue to rise, the Clinton administration undertook a wave of new military training programs in Africa.

Between 1991-1998, U.S. weapons and training deliveries to Africa totalled more than $227 million. In 1998 alone, direct weapons transfers and IMET training totalled $20.1 million. And, under the Pentagon's Joint Combined Exchange Training (JCET) program, U.S. special forces have trained military personnel from at least 34 of Africa's 53 nations, including troops fighting on both sides of the DRC's civil war from Rwanda and Uganda supporting the rebels to Zimbabwe and Namibia (supporting the Kabila regime). Even as it fuels military build-up, the U.S. continues cutting development assistance to Africa and remains unable or unwilling to promote alternative non-violent forms of engagement.

While the U.S. ranks number one in global weapons exports, it falls dead last among industrialized nations in providing non-military foreign aid to the developing world. In 1997, the U.S. devoted only 0.09% of GNP to international development assistance, the lowest proportion of all developed countries. U.S. development aid to all of sub-Saharan Africa dropped to just $700 million in recent years. By restricting the flow of weapons and training and increasing support for sustainable development policies, the U.S. could help create the conditions needed for peace and stability to take root.

Although Congress recently passed legislation requiring the President to begin negotiations toward an international arms sales code of conduct based on human rights, non-aggression, and democracy, the U.S. continues to exempt its own exports from these same standards. The Clinton should have made good on its acclaimed commitments to human rights and democracy by supporting passage of the bipartisan McKinney-Rohrabacher Code of Conduct on Arms Transfers, a measure which would take U.S. weapons out of the hands of dictators and human rights abusers.

The American should instead provide increased unconditional debt forgiveness to African nations and encourage them to shift resources away from military build-up and toward human development. The U.S. should immediately forgive the hundreds of millions of dollars in military debt accrued by governments in Zaire, the Sudan, and Somalia. It should also take steps toward further debt relief by passing the HOPE for Africa bill introduced by Rep. Jesse Jackson, Jr. in the House and Sen. Russell Feingold in the Senate.

The U.S. should provide increased development assistance to Africa and encourage civil-society building. Moreover, the U.S. has failed to acknowledge its own role in fueling conflict and undermining democratic development in Africa. A July 1999 Report by the U.S. Bureau of Intelligence and Research states clearly that "Arms transfers and trafficking and the conflicts they feed are having a devastating impact on Sub-Saharan Africa." Yet, the authors fail to attribute responsibility to the U.S. for either its past or current military weapons and training exports to Africa, explicitly leaving the U.S. out of the picture: "Arms suppliers in Western and Eastern Europe, the Middle East, North America, Latin America, and Asia have sold arms to African clients." In fact, nowhere does the report mention U.S. arms transfers to the region, although more than $20 million worth of U.S. weapons and training were delivered to Africa in 1998 alone.

Nor is there any recognition that the hundreds of millions of dollars' worth of U.S. equipment transferred to the Mobutu regime in Zaire and Jonas Savimbi's UNITA movement in Angola since the 1970's are still being utilized in current African conflicts today. American policy toward the provision of arms and training to African military forces point out that the United States is not the primary supplier of weaponry to the region, and that in any case U.S. military programs in Africa are designed to promote peacekeeping and professionalism, not proliferation and war.

The U.S. have strengthened the military capabilities of combatants involved in some of Africa's most violent and intractable conflicts. As to the relative importance of U.S. arms transfers to Africa, data from the most recent edition of the U.S. Arms Control and Disarmament Agency's publication, World Military Expenditures and Arms Transfers, ranks the U.S. as the second leading arms supplier to both Central Africa behind China and ahead of France and Southern Africa which is behind Russia tied for second with France. In contrast, the most recent data from the Congressional Research Service suggests that at best the United States ranks sixth in arms transfers to Africa for the period from 1995-1998, after China, Russia, the United Kingdom, France, and Italy.

The U.S. Military assistance in Africa's First World War in 1998, U.S. weapons to Africa totalled $12.5 million, including substantial deliveries to Chad, Namibia, and Zimbabwe all now backing Kabila. On the rebel side, Uganda received nearly $1.5 million in weaponry over the past two years, and Rwanda was importing U.S. weapons as late as 1993 (one year before the brutal genocide erupted). U.S. military transfers in the form of direct government-to-government weapons deliveries, commercial sales, and IMET training to the states directly involved has totalled more than $125 million since the end of the Cold War. How many African military personal received military training in America Angola 31,000 + 31 000; Burundi 74,000 + 312,000+386,000; Chad 21,767,000+24,677,000+46,444,000; DRC 15,151,000+218,000+15,369,000; Namibia 2,311,000+1,934,000+4,245,000; Rwanda 324,000+324,000; Sudan 30,258,000+1,815,000+32,073,000; Uganda 1,517,000+9,903,000+11,420,000; Zimbabwe 567,000+828,000+1,395,000 TOTAL 71,969,000+39,718,000+ USA Dollars $111,687,000

Post-Cold War International Military Education and Training (IMET) to Countries Involved in the Congo War, 1989-1998 (constant 1998 dollars) Country Source: Department of Defense, Foreign Military Sales, Foreign Military Construction Sales and Military Assistance Facts, Foreign Military Sales, Construction, and Assistance Facts as of September 1998, (Washington, DC: U.S. Department of Defense, 1999). Although detailed reports of the fighting are difficult to confirm, U.S. military hardware was no doubt being used as the violence spread. During the height of the war, the New York Times reported the use of U.S. communications equipment by the rebels, and small arms like the U.S.-designed M-16 combat rifle, often circulating from past wars, have been used in both combat and civilian attacks.

Heavier equipment and training transferred to the region by the U.S. has also likely contributed to both sides of the war. Uganda, which received just under a million dollars in U.S. weapons in 1997 (up from $64,000 in 1996), boosted its total military expenditure in 1999 from $150 million to $350 million, increasing troop commitments and stockpiling tanks and antiaircraft missiles for use against Kabila's forces. Zimbabwe and Angola both recipients of U.S. training and equipment also sent jets, tanks, and troops into the combat. Because many U.S. supplied weapons have outlasted the governments and conflicts for which they were intended, yesterday's supplies are finding new uses today. Last March a Belgian arms dealer was arrested in South Africa for selling 8,000 U.S. M16 rifles from Vietnam War era arsenals to Kabila's forces. In fact, many of the illicit arms traffickers working in Central Africa got their start as covert operators for the U.S.

From her work investigating and interviewing illicit weapons dealers in Africa, Kathi Austin has documented a number of U.S.-sponsored smugglers working in the region, noting that "little attention is paid to how weapon suppliers fan the flames of the region's conflicts." Last spring, four U.S. citizens claiming to be Christian missionaries were arrested in Zimbabwe for attempting to smuggle small arms caches which included sniper rifles, shotguns, machine guns, firearms, telescopic sights, knives, camouflage cream, two-way radios and ammunition across national borders. U.S. policy has done so well in helping create a demand for weapons in the developing world, and the industry has been so eager to fill it, that the arms market is taking on a life of its own, largely outside government regulations and civilian oversight.

"We need a simple and transparent set of rules to govern all our military education programs. The first rule should be that the United States does not give any kind of military assistance whatever to governments that murder their own people." Rep. Chris Smith Subcommittee on International Operations and Human Rights, July 1998.

U.S. military training now takes a number of forms in Africa, including traditional International Military Education Training (IMET), Expanded IMET (E-IMET), Joint Combined Exchange Training (JCET), and more recent training under the African Crisis Response Initiative (ACRI). IMET training for Africa has floated between $4-8 million throughout the 1990s.

In 1998, the U.S. provided $5.8 million in IMET training for over 400 African soldiers. As Congress has cut IMET funding in recent years, however, the other programs appear to have sprouted up to fill the gaps and further strengthen military-to-military relations between the U.S. and Africa. This year, the Department of Defense has also established the Africa Center for Strategic Studies (ACSS), which allegedly provides "academic" rather than tactical or operational instruction in "civil-military relations, national security strategy, and defense economics."

JCET programs, which use special operations forces, remain exempt from congressional oversight and have only begun to be reported in detail to Congress and the public. From 1995-1998 U.S. special forces conducted JCET training in at least 34 of the 53 African countries, including Namibia, Rwanda, Uganda, and Zimbabwe all fighting in the DRC as well as Mozambique, Cote d'Ivorie, Equatorial Guinea, Ghana, Guinea-Bissau, Malawi, Mali, Mauritania, Morocco, Senegal, Sierra Leone, Tunisia, Cameroon, Botswana. Although the number of troops trained under JCET is difficult to track, at least 9,100 host nation military personnel participated in the program worldwide in 1997. Despite the Pentagon's claims that JCET helps "enhance host nation skills" and increase the U.S.'s "long-term...influence in the participating countries," little evidence exists to suggest that these programs fulfil their official purpose. They may in fact be contributing to counterinsurgency and human rights violations.

When Rwandan soldiers invaded the former Zaire in 1996, attacking refugee camps and massacring civilians, the U.S. was caught having to defend the special operations training that had been underway with Rwandan troops. Although U.S. officials had claimed the training was devoted to human rights, the Washington Post later reported that Rwandan troops were being trained in combat as well. As the Post concluded, "U.S. promotion of human rights has been overshadowed by questions about whether Rwandan units trained by Americans later participated in atrocities in the war in Zaire." A number of Members of Congress, including Rep. Christopher Smith (R-NJ) who chairs the House subcommittee on international operations and human rights, have questioned whether the Pentagon is even attempting to find out if troops trained under JCET have been involved in human rights violations.

In 1997, the Department of Defense instituted the African Crisis Response Initiative (ACRI), a scaled down version of the African Crisis Response Force (ACRF) that was originally proposed and began calling for more anti-narcotics operations in the region. ACRI's stated purpose is to "work in partnership with African countries to enhance their capacity to respond to humanitarian crises and peacekeeping challenges in a timely and effective manner.... to assist Africans in developing rapidly deployable, interoperable battalions from stable democratic countries." However, the program has been criticized by analysts in both the U.S. and Africa for contributing to counter-insurgency operations or conventional warfare by the trained troops and providing yet another mechanism for channeling U.S. military training and equipment to favored regimes. Some view the program as no more than an insurance policy against U.S. involvement in peacekeeping operations in the region again.

As Daniel Volman, director of the Africa Research Project, has noted, "While the scope and scale of the ACRI program are quite limited, a number of important questions about the impact of the program and about future involvement of the United States in peacekeeping operations and other kinds of military activities in Africa remain unanswered....The declared intent of the program is to enhance the capability of African forces to conduct peacekeeping operations. But much of the training and equipment provided can also enhance their capability to engage in counter-insurgency operations or conventional warfare with other states."

Under ACRI, the U.S. is providing about $8.1 million in grants to 39 African countries for military education and training, including Uganda, South Africa, Eritrea, and Ethiopia. Ethiopia and Eritrea have been engaged in a bloody on-again, off-again border war since May of 1998. In January 2000, the conflict threatened to heat up again as Ethiopian Prime Minister Meles Zenawi denounced the terms of a U.S. supported peace plan.

Meanwhile, military units trained by the U.S. continue to be involved in human rights abuses and counter-insurgency efforts. In 1998, Ugandan troops trained under the new ACRI program were re-deployed a week later as part of a major counter-insurgency campaign against the Allied Democratic Forces in western Uganda.

The Clinton administration's latest undertaking, the Africa Center for Security Studies (ACSS) defines its mission as follows: to "support democratic governance in Africa by offering senior African civil and military leaders a rigorous academic and practical program in civil-military relations, national security strategy, and defense economics."The program will be paid for by U.S. tax dollars and plans to commence operations in November of this year with a two-week seminar in Dakar, Senegal. DoD operates similar centers for other regional allies around the world.

Although ACSS has yet to be seen in action, critics argue that once again the U.S. is focusing its resources in the wrong arenas, promoting military relationships at the expense of democracy-building and conflict prevention. Clarissa Kayosa of Demilitarization for Democracy and the Year 2000 Campaign to Redirect World Military Spending to Human Development has noted that "While many African focused organizations in the United States agree on the need for a professional, law abiding, rights respecting, civilian controlled armed forces, U.S. military training in other parts of the world, including Africa, has mixed results at best....Africa is in a state of collapse now and what it needs is not more military assistance but more development assistance.

African Militaries Trained by the U.S., 1997-98 are Angola; Ghana; Rwanda; Benin; Guinea; Sao Tome & Principe; Botswana; Guinea-Bissau; Senegal; Cameroon; Ivory Coast; Seychelles; Cape Verde; Kenya; Sierra Leone; Central African Republic; Lesotho; South Africa; Chad; Madagascar; Swaziland; Comoros; Malawi; Tanzania; Congo (Braz.); Mali; Togo; Cote d'Ivoirie; Mauritania; Tunisia; Djibouti; Mozambique; Uganda; Eritrea; Namibia; Zambia; Ethiopia; Niger and Zimbabwe.

As Demilitarization for Democracy (DfD) has noted, the military's hold on political and economic power continues to undermine democratic transition in many African nations today. In a 1997 report, DfD found that 57% of African countries are clearly not democratic, and that the armed forces still hold substantial political and economic power in 40 of the 53 African nations. Yet, from 1991-1995, the U.S. provided military assistance to 50 countries in Africa, 94% of the nations on the continent. Although military assistance to Africa began to decline in the early 1990s, more recent years have seen new increases in training and weapons exports. Between 1991-1998, U.S. weapons and training deliveries to Africa totalled more than $227 million.

Because many of the recipient countries remain some of the world's poorest, the U.S. government provided around $87 million in foreign military financing loans (subsidized by U.S. taxpayer dollars) to cover the costs, increasing the debt burden that is already suffocating the continent. The DRC alone owes more than $150 million in outstanding DoD loans, with Liberia, Somalia, and Sudan owing another $160 million combined. These loans, accrued while corrupt dictators were serving as U.S. clients, have further contributed to the economic hardships of these nations by saddling them with unproductive military debt.

In an article titled "Why the U.S. Won't Help," a Nairobi newspaper recently explained, "Right from the days of the Cold War, Western governments have been comfortable with a situation in which African regimes squandered meagre resources on the instruments of war, borrowing from the West to finance domestic consumption. The war in the Congo and the countries involved in it are a case in point." DfD's report cited "reduced political and economic power of armed forces" as a main element of democracy embraced by the African NGO community. Were the U.S. also contributing to civil society building and sustainable development efforts, perhaps its efforts to strengthen African militaries would seem less hypocritical. However, U.S. non-military development aid to Africa continues to face serious cuts even as the continent's debt grows, and its economic future remains bleak. In recent years, U.S. development aid to all of sub-Saharan Africa has dropped to around $700 million. In 1995, Congress cut development assistance to Africa by 25%, following the elimination of funding in previous years for the Development Fund for Africa, a program which supports sustainable development projects.

Three years later, in 1998, no funds were specifically earmarked for Africa from the meager $1.8 billion in total development funding allocated in the U.S. budget, leaving the world's poorest countries competing for scarce funds. In 1997, the U.S. devoted only 0.09% of GNP to international development assistance, the lowest proportion of all developed countries. Only 20% of that aid went to the world's least developed nations. While the U.S. ranks number one in global weapons exports, it falls dead last among industrialized nations in providing non-military foreign aid to the developing world.

Still, critics will argue that U.S. military weapons and training to Africa remain at a negligible level in relation to international arms transfers. At approximately $20.1 million in 1998, the amount of direct weapons sales and IMET training to all of Africa constitutes only a small fraction of the $12-15 billion in U.S. military exports transferred globally every year. The numbers do pale in comparison to the more than $500 million in U.S. weapons that went to Egypt or the $1 billion to Israel in 1998 alone. But then perhaps the question should be one of good policy and long-term consequences rather than comparative statistics. As a November State Department report on arms flows to Central Africa recognized, "Although the infusion of weapons to this region is small compared with arms transfers in the rest of the world, the impact of such trafficking on the politically fragile Central Africa/Great Lakes region has been catastrophic." Ironically, U.S. weapons sales were not mentioned in the report.

"The time is long past when one could claim ignorance about what was happening in Africa or about what was needed to achieve progress. The time is also past when the responsibility for producing change could be shifted onto others' shoulders. It is ours and it is theirs the world's and Africa's." Ex UN General Secretary Kofi Annan

Yet, real action is not on the agenda. Military training programs continue to promulgate, weapons sales to the developing world are on the rise, and small arms manufacturers are looking to increase exports worldwide. Although U.S. arms manufacturers often boast of making the world a safer place and the Pentagon rallies around human rights training for foreign militaries, history teaches a different lesson. Unless the U.S. recognizes and begins to remedy the mistakes of the past, the uncontrolled transfer of military equipment and training will continue to impede human development and undermine efforts toward a sustainable peace, in Africa and around the world.

Arms control critics will no doubt continue to argue that "Guns don't kill people; people kill people." (Interesting point considering some of the people the U.S. has armed to the hilt.) The Rwandan genocide of 1994, inflicted largely with machetes, rocks, and other non-military weapons, is often touted as proof that arms control just doesn't work. Ultimately, however, those arguments ignore the long-term political, economic, and social effects of flooding the developing world with deadly weaponry and military training.

While the U.S. has recently begun to call for stronger monitoring and policing mechanisms to limit illicit weapons trafficking, the government continues to focus on the demand side of sales rather than its own contributions as a major weapons supplier.

Certainly, the U.S. arms trade has not been the sole cause of conflict in Africa. However, the weapons and resources that are available to parties involved in a conflict do play a critical role in determining whether a dispute will evolve into violence, and, if so, how long and devastating that violence will be. Moreover, as Africans work to overcome the problems of corrupt governments and a growing culture of violence, the international community has a responsibility to support those efforts through policies that promote sustainable development and peaceful nation-building rather than augmenting existing instabilities with uncontrolled arms trade policies.

The hypocrisy of asking Africa to develop and democratize while shrinking levels of non-military international aid and increasing weapons and training to the continent does not seem to have registered with policy-makers. To demonstrate real commitment to developing a new partnership with Africa, the U.S. needs to redirect the focus away from strengthening military capacity and toward promoting human development in Africa.

The world is awash with weapons. From Syria and Iraq, to the deserts of the Sahel, to the Nigerian bush, it's a good time to be a guerrilla fighter in no small part because it's so outrageously easy to acquire the kind of weaponry necessary to carry out insurgent warfare. That fact of 21st century life is made clear by the most recent edition of the Small Arms Survey: Weapons and the World, a report that found the value of the global small arms trade has nearly doubled between 2001 and 2011. Since then, it has continued to increase, with just over $5 billion in arms transferred in 2012. Because of the opaque nature of the global small arms market the full total may very well be higher.

The half-hearted embargo by the EU, and similar efforts by Washington to apply pressure on Cairo by withholding advanced weapons shipments, illustrate how a country such as Egypt can insulate itself from political pressure delivered by its arms suppliers. As the report notes, these efforts in Western capitals resulted in Egypt looking elsewhere for weapons, including exploring the possibility of an arms agreement with Russia.

But examining the role that international arms transfers are playing to fuel violence in other post-Arab Spring states is an effort severely undermined by the lack of transparency governing such shipments. Since civil war arrived in Syria in 2011, several world powers have attempted to curtail arms shipments destined for forces loyal to President Bashar al-Assad. Nonetheless, the report notes that media accounts indicate that Russia, Iran, and North Korea continue to supply the regime with weaponry. While the EU has imposed an arms embargo, Russia has blocked the creation of a similar U.N. measure.

While the Small Arms Survey advocates for restraint in supplying weapons to these unstable regions, several Western governments have nonetheless provided arms to rebel groups seen as allies against either extremist groups or repressive regimes. Western arms shipments to Kurdish Peshmerga forces, for example, present significant risks both of misuse and that they will end up in the wrong hands. Case in point: When U.S. fighter jets dropped crates of weapons to Kurdish forces besieged in the Syrian city of Kobani, some of the lethal supplies were picked up by the Islamic State. In other cases, Syrian rebel groups have obtained U.S.-supplied weapons after the materiel was put on the black market by the Iraqi troops for whom they were intended.

Other weaponry supplied to Syria's rebels have their origin in the huge arms stockpiles left behind by the Soviet Union. Throughout South Eastern Europe, arms stockpiles left over from the Soviet era on the one hand present opportunities for export Croatian arms have, for example, been purchased and funnelled toward rebels friendly toward the United States. On the other hand, such stockpiles pose life-threatening risks for the local population. According to the Small Arms Survey, 51 explosions occurred at munitions sites in South Eastern Europe between 1980 and 2014, resulting in more than 700 casualties.

Many Balkan states have moved to reduce the size of these arms stockpiles, which are poorly maintained and catalogued. But that effort has been undermined by commercial priorities. Many states, according to the Small Arms Survey, are loathed to destroy weapons before they have tested their "marketability." Others "simply do not know the precise quantities of ammunition (whether surplus or operational) in their stockpiles, often because of poor stockpile accounting practices," the report notes. That lack of oversight makes the weapons ripe for theft or illicit sale.

Perhaps nowhere has the proliferation of Cold War-era weapons been more acutely felt than in Mali, where the government, with the support of France, has for the last three years sought to put down a separatist rebellion that has seen an influx of jihadi fighters and groups. It is often said that the Malian conflict was fuelled by weaponry funnelled from the stores of toppled Libyan strongman Muammar al-Qaddafi. While Malian rebel fighters gained combat experience in the conflict that led to his downfall, and returned to Mali with large amounts of weapons, the Small Arms Survey found that the bulk of the weapons used in the uprising there were in fact seized from Malian government stores.

Ammunition examined in Mali indicates these weapons were mostly supplied by China and the Soviet Union. Qaddafi's arms store instead provided a qualitative edge for insurgent fighters in Mali. "A scarcity of heavy machine guns and related ammunition was reportedly overcome through Libyan-sourced materiel," the report notes. "Libya is a prominent source of the larger-calibre weapons that were observed in insurgent hands in 2012, including vehicle mounted ZU-23-2-pattern anti-aircraft auto-cannon, employed primarily to engage ground targets. Likewise, Libya served as a source of MANPADS and their missiles that are now in the possession of jihadists in northern Mali." (MANPADS refers to man-portable air defense systems and are typically shoulder fired missiles that can engage aerial targets flying at low to medium altitudes.) If there's a lesson to be had from the voluminous Small Arms Survey, it's arguably this: The weapons supplied to friendly client states today have a nasty habit of reappearing in the hands of unexpected enemies 10, 20, or 30 years from now.

The McKinney-Rohrabacher Code of Conduct on Arms Transfers (HR 2269), a measure which would take U.S. weapons out of the hands of dictators and human rights abusers, passed the House in 1997. That bill has been reintroduced in the 106th Congress but has not yet received enough support for final passage. In November 1999, Congress did pass a limited measure that requires the President to begin negotiations on an international code of conduct based on human rights, democracy, and non-aggression. However, this legislation does not condition U.S. sales on these basic standards. In order to legitimately press for an international arms trade regime, the U.S. needs to take unilateral steps as well. Both the House and Senate should commit to passing the full McKinney-Rohrabacher Code of Conduct in 2000, and President Clinton should sign the bill into law before his term closes.

Congress should take also immediate steps to close the loopholes in Joint Combined Exchange Training (JCET) and other training programs by passing the International Military Training Transparency and Accountability Act (HR 1063). This bill, introduced by Rep. Chris Smith (R-NJ) and supported by a strong bi-partisan coalition, would prohibit all forms of military training and services to countries that are already ineligible for International Military Education Training (IMET). All U.S. military training programs should receive congressional oversight and approval, with effective mechanisms in place for reviewing and assessing their impact on human rights and democratic consolidation in the recipient countries. Promoting Human Development International debt relief that is not conditioned on unproven and often damaging structural adjustment programs has become a necessary prerequisite for peace and development in Africa.

President Clinton and Congress should commit to unconditional debt relief and encourage civil society-building in Africa by immediately forgiving all military debt accrued by governments no longer in power and by passing the HOPE for Africa bill as introduced by Rep. Jesse Jackson, Jr. This bill offers the most comprehensive debt relief and human development policy currently under consideration in Congress. President Clinton should also commit to the Jubilee 2000 campaign's call for developing a plan this year, in conjunction with local non-governmental organizations and civil society, for full and unconditional debt relief. Finally, at the very least, the Administration and Congress should restore the previous level of $800 million in development assistance to Africa in the FY2001 budget. This level of funding should serve as the floor not the ceiling for future aid packages. The U.S. should further strive to raise African development funding to $2 billion by 2003 and consult directly with non-governmental institutions to ensure that funds are dispersed and used appropriately. The negligible amount of aid provided each year for African development can only be called disgraceful in comparison to the billions spent each year on the U.S. arms trade. In times of budget crises, increased military spending, and a pull from many toward greater isolationism, creating real change in U.S.-Africa relations will require a demanding public, as well as effective leadership.

At a press briefing in November, Assistant Secretary of State for African Affairs Susan Rice was asked poignantly by a journalist, "I am curious as to why you think that the men and women of the Congo should believe, especially given the United States' long history of involvement in the Congo in support of Mobutu – why should the men and women of the Congo believe that the U.S. really has the Congo's interests at heart?"

Until the U.S. is willing to serve the interests of long-term peace and stability, rather than short-term profit and politics, its Cold War policies will live on in Africa wreaking destruction in places like the DRC, Angola, and Sierra Leone, Eritrea and Ethiopia. In November 1999, the State Department concluded: "Arms trafficking to the Central Africa/Great Lakes region will continue unabated for the foreseeable future," noting that, "restricting arms flows to the region will require an unprecedented demonstration of sustained political will on the part of the regional and international leaders." By shifting a mere fraction of the energy that currently goes to strengthen African militaries toward non-military alternatives that could promote democracy, development, and peacebuilding, the United States could make a significant contribution to providing that leadership and promoting security and stability in the region. We should embark on that path of change now, before the potential for positive engagement in the future is lost to the legacies of the past.

The collapse of the Soviet bloc saw a new flood of small arms entering Africa as manufacturers put additional millions of surplus Cold War-era weapons on the international arms market at cut-rate prices. Years later, these durable killing machines fight on in the hands of insurgents, local militias, criminal organizations and ordinary people left vulnerable to violence by ineffective policing and simmering civil conflict. In some parts of Africa, a Soviet-designed AK-47 assault rifle, coveted for its simplicity and firepower, can be purchased for as little as $6, or traded for a chicken or sack of grain. In 1999 the Red Cross estimated that in the Somali capital of Mogadishu alone, the city's 1.3 million residents possessed over a million guns among an estimated 550 mm small arms in circulation worldwide. The widespread abuse of weapons diverts scarce government resources from health and education to public security, discourages investment and economic growth, and deprives developing countries of the skills and talents of the victims of small arms.

"The proliferation of light weapons in Africa poses a major threat to development," noted Ms. Virginia Gamba, the former director of the Arms Management Programme of the South African Institute for Security Studies (ISS). Their low cost, ease of use and availability "may escalate conflicts, undermine peace agreements, intensify the violence and impact of crime, impede economic and social development and hinder the development of social stability, democracy and good governance." In July 2001 the US government estimated that small arms are fuelling conflicts in 22 African countries that have taken 7-8 million lives. In Africa guns are not just the weapons of choice but also weapons of mass destruction.

When weapons outlast wars. The development impact of war on individuals, communities and states is unambiguous and well documented. By its nature and sometimes by design modern warfare destroys economic and social infrastructure, uproots populations, paralyses economic activity, disrupts vital health and education services and diverts financial resources from development to defence. Less well understood is the impact of small arms on development in post-conflict situations. Unlike heavy weapons systems, which can be costly to acquire and operate and comparatively easy to decommission or monitor, the end of a war does not necessarily bring an end to the use of light weapons.

As Robert Muggah and Peter Bachelor, analysts for the Small Arms Survey, a European research institute, report in a recent study, Development Held Hostage: Assessing the Effects of Small Arms on Human Development, "the durability of small arms ensures that once they are present in a country they present a continuous risk especially in societies where there are large accumulations of weapons.... They frequently outlast peace agreements and are taken up again in the post-conflict period" by criminal gangs, vigilantes, dissidents, and individuals concerned about personal security. In areas where state security is weak or absent, possession of a gun can be a matter of survival, either to seize food and other vital resources or as protection from attack. In other places the low cost and ready availability of firearms can promote what experts call a "culture of violence," where gun ownership becomes a symbol of power and status, and gun violence a first resort for the settlement of personal and political disputes. Rebels in Sierra Leone: small arms not only take many lives, but also exact a heavy toll on African societies and economies.

South Africa has suffered considerably from the misuse of small arms since the end of apartheid in 1994 and has moved aggressively to reduce their availability. Unlike most other African countries, South Africa has a large number of small arms in legal circulation, with over 4 mn guns registered to private, primarily white, owners at the end of 1999. In common with countries bordering conflict areas in West and East Africa, however, South Africa has also suffered from the illegal influx from neighbouring states of weapons that have outlasted the wars they were intended to fight.

In the 1970s, the apartheid government began supplying thousands of tons of arms and ammunition to its domestic and regional allies for the defence of white minority rule. An estimated 30 tonnes of guns and explosives were smuggled into the country by the anti-apartheid movements, which also left arms stockpiles at their base camps in surrounding countries. As many as 4 mn weapons from various sources have illegally found their way into the hands of South African civilians. The presence of so many weapons outside government control has overwhelmed law enforcement efforts, contributed to crime and public insecurity, hampered economic growth and caused tragic and avoidable deaths and injuries.

Measuring the effects, assessing the peacetime impact of small arms on South Africa and other African countries is difficult. Many countries lack the capacity to collect and analyse data about the use of small arms. Moreover, many of the greatest costs to development, such as deferred investment, reduced economic activity and lost productivity due to injury and insecurity, are indirect, and therefore hard to measure.

One of the best indicators, said Dr. Etienne Krug, director of the World Health Organization (WHO), Injuries and Violence Prevention Department, are public health records. But particularly in developing regions like Africa, WHO cautions in its 2001 report Small Arms and Global Health, "data on the impact of small arms on the health of individuals are far from complete." Statistics are vital for the development of effective strategies to meet the medical challenges of guns, he noted, but donors are often unwilling to fund data collection as part of health projects.

Globally, WHO put the number of violent deaths from all causes in 1998 at 2.3 million. Several hundred thousand of these are believed to be gunshot victims: 42 per cent as a result of suicide, 32 per cent by murder and 26 per cent by war. The study found a correlation between gun violence and development: death rates in low and middle-income countries, at 42 per 100,000 people, were more than double the 17 per 100,000 rate found in high-income countries.

Many hundreds of thousands more people survive gun injuries but require costly medical care and often suffer permanent physical and emotional disabilities. The absence of sophisticated emergency medical facilities, however, means that far more gunshot injuries prove fatal to victims in developing countries than in the industrialized North. The direct cost can be high. A 1997 study of 1,000 gunshot victims in South Africa put the total cost of hospital treatment at nearly R30 mn (then $6.5 mn). The indirect impact of gun violence on public health systems, asserts WHO, also is huge. Treating large numbers of patients with gunshot wounds "has a draining effect on basic health care and diverts much-needed resources from other health and social services." Crime rates rising, crime statistics can also provide a measurement of the impact of small arms on development. Because apartheid-era crime reports in South Africa are considered unreliable, ISS researchers analyzed post-apartheid police records and reported a "marked increase" in the use of firearms to commit murder, from 41.5 per cent of homicides in 1994 to 49.3 per cent in 1998, even as the overall number of murders decreased.

The use of small arms in robberies also increased significantly, from 51,000 incidents in 1996 to 69,500 in 1998, although the overall number of robberies involving weapons of all kinds increased only marginally. The increase, the analysts argue, "shows that more criminals are arming themselves" and that "access to firearms has become easier compared to previous years." By 2000 the South African government found that homicide, primarily involving firearms, was the leading cause of death among young men aged 15-21 and that gunshots from all causes (murder, suicide and accidents) were the single largest cause of non-natural death in the country.

The death and injury of so many young people have profound consequences for development reducing the number of educated people entering the work force, diverting family and social resources into the care of those disabled by gun violence and forcing the government to redirect funding from social services to law enforcement. Last year, for example, South Africa spent $1.96 bn on law enforcement and $1.56 bn on health.

In Kenya, the illegal influx of small arms from surrounding states appears to be fuelling violence far from the volatile northern border areas. The increased availability of weapons in Nairobi, for example, may be a factor in the rising number of murders and the use of violence in burglaries, although Kenyan police report that the number of reported robberies themselves has declined. A recent survey by the UN Centre for Human Settlements (Habitat) and the Kenyan government found that 75 per cent of city residents felt insecure at night despite an increased police presence in high crime areas.

Men, women and guns, the disproportionate impact of weapons on young men has been widely noted in conflict situations. Much the same is true in peacetime. According to WHO, males of all ages comprise 80 per cent of homicide victims and males are 3 to 6 times more likely than females to commit murder, with both victims and assailants drawn largely from the ranks of men aged 18-49.

Even where guns are not widely used, said UN Children's Fund (UNICEF) small arms project officer Ms. Lieke van de Wiel, "the social fabric of society really changes if the weapons are present. If you go to the post office and the man next to you has a gun, you feel much less secure. It's the power issue." The implicit threat of violence, Ms. Van de Wiel noted, is particularly frightening for women. "If there are men around with guns, whether they use them or not, women are intimidated. The threat is in the air."

The governments of some of the African countries most affected by gun violence, including Mali and South Africa, are moving aggressively to challenge the culture of violence with the strong support of their civil societies and the UN. In South Africa, according to statistics from a non-governmental advocacy group, Gun Free South Africa, 12 per cent of gun death victims in 1998 were female and about 7 per cent were under the age of 17. While the limited data available shows that the overwhelming majority of female victims were murdered by domestic partners or ex-partners, evidence that small arms are a major factor in domestic violence in Africa is more elusive.

Researchers in Tanzania reported that guns were involved in 6 per cent of domestic violence cases, while a study in Zambia found that firearms were used in the murder of just three victims of domestic violence in 1995. The actual incidence, however, is almost certainly higher, as violent crimes against women are less likely to be reported and recording the type of weapon used is rarely a priority.

While gun manufacturers argue that small arms are ideal self-defence weapons for women equalizers in a fight with larger and more powerful men males continue to exercise a near-monopoly on the ownership and control of weapons. Far from liberating women from the fear of violence, the ready availability of guns makes matters worse. "Women feel threatened by it," Ms. Van de Wiel said, "men feel empowered by it."

"You can run away from physical abuse," one South African woman told a journalist in 1998. "But you can't run away from bullets." Challenging the 'culture of violence' Part of the challenge of reducing both the availability and the use of small arms in South Africa, writes sociologist Dr. Jacklyn Cock, is that apartheid and the struggle against it has created a "culture of violence" that legitimizes the use of guns to resolve disputes, further polarizes social relations among races, classes and sexes, and creates a demand for arms that is supplied both legally and illicitly. Such a culture, argues WHO, "may dictate whether or not the weapons are actually used. In other words, in some societies it may be more socially acceptable to use firearms than in others. This factor may explain why in some societies guns are available but are used less than in others."

The cultural significance of the AK-47 to the formerly colonized peoples of Southern Africa is a case in point. After decades of use by anti-colonial and anti-apartheid movements, the powerful weapon has come to be associated with liberation. A silhouette of the gun figures prominently on the Mozambican flag. Freedom songs from the struggles against minority rule in Namibia, South Africa, Zimbabwe and Angola often extolled its virtues, and those of the fighters carrying it. In some African countries today, however, the weapon and its US and European equivalent equips brutal insurgencies, criminal gangs and paramilitary militias -- paralyzing development efforts and dangerously exaggerating the association between arms and masculinity that is common to many cultures around the world.

Replacing the romantic image of guns with an appreciation of their destructive impact, advocates argue, will require a long-term effort to reduce the supply, improve police protection and increase educational and economic opportunities for young men to break their identification with guns and violence.

The governments of some of the African countries most affected by gun violence, including Mali and South Africa, are moving aggressively to challenge the culture of violence with the strong support of their civil societies and the UN. In 1995 the South African and Mozambican governments began joint operations to curtail the flow of apartheid-era weapons entering South Africa illegally from former war zones in Mozambique. By the end of 1998, a series of missions, dubbed "Operations Rachel," had located and destroyed over 400 tonnes of light weapons and over 40 mm rounds of ammunition in one of the most effective arms decommissioning exercises in the world.

Several months later the South African government announced that it would destroy domestic stocks of surplus and confiscated weapons instead of selling them. The new programme, Operation Mouflon, formally began on 6 July 2000 with the destruction of some 63,000 assault rifles, pistols and machine guns, among nearly 263,000 small arms scheduled for destruction.

Bonfires in Mali in West Africa, the government of Malian President Alpha Oumar Konaré and the UN Development Programme collected and publicly destroyed over 3,000 weapons in a bonfire on 27 March 1996. That action was followed by the adoption, on 31 October 1998, of a three-year moratorium on the import of light weapons into the region by the Economic Community of West African States (ECOWAS). The organization also established some arms register and database. The Organization of African Unity (OAU) followed suit in 1999, condemning the illicit proliferation and trafficking in small arms and calling for coordinated African action against the trade. Although the ECOWAS moratorium was extended for an additional three years in July 2001, a lack of resources for enforcement of both the West African and OAU initiatives has limited their effectiveness. The South African government and its non-governmental allies have focused on community-based efforts to reduce the allure of small arms. One of the most successful programmes has been the Soweto-based Youth Against Crime, formed by students to educate their peers about the dangers of small arms violence.

Acting in cooperation with the police and Gun Free South Africa, 21 Soweto schools have declared their premises gun free. Efforts are now underway to launch the campaign nationally through the umbrella South African Youth Council. ISS researchers have also surveyed community attitudes towards the ownership and use of firearms in order to design more effective education and disarmament programmes. They found that the great majority of people viewed small arms as an important contributor to crime and violence.

But they also discovered, among nearly 60 per cent of respondents, a willingness to carry one for self-defence. This reflects a residual distrust of the police among African, Asian and mixed race ("coloured") South Africans from the days when the police were seen as the enforcers of apartheid, analysts say. But it also reflects a popular perception, sometimes apparently exaggerated, that there has been an uncontrolled surge of criminal and vigilante violence since the end of white rule in 1994. There is strong public support both for tougher gun control laws and more and better-trained police to enforce them.

Alleviating poverty, inequality. In much the same way that the disarmament, demobilization and re-integration of former soldiers is now considered essential to the success of peace-building efforts in conflict situations, the Small Arms Survey notes, "interventions to curb the demand for small arms should focus on the alleviation of poverty and structural inequality, thereby helping to reduce some of the factors prompting people to keep or acquire weapons" in post-conflict societies. In the view of virtually all the experts, neither poverty, injustice nor the availability of cheap powerful small arms is sufficient to explain gun violence. It is at the intersection of all three, they say, that guns from past wars find new owners and new victims for Africa's open graves. Helping children say 'no' to guns Access to automatic rifles by itself does not create child soldiers, UN Children's Fund (UNICEF) small arms project officer Ms. Lieke van de Wiel told Africa Recovery, but "the use of small arms does change their role. Small arms are small and easy to handle, so any kid becomes a professional killer in no time." In earlier conflicts, she noted, children might have carried supplies or been placed in forward positions to draw enemy fire away from other soldiers. With powerful modern firearms, however, "They can be effective killers right away." In places saturated with weapons, "Children don't necessarily know guns are dangerous," Ms. van de Wiel explained. "Parents have them in the home so children are exposed to them all the time. If small arms are in the daily lives of children, they must learn how to minimize the risk."

In 2002 UNICEF will launch a pilot programme to help adolescents learn about the danger of small arms and alternatives to gun violence in Somalia, Liberia, Kosovo and Tajikistan. The project will build on UNICEF's work with existing youth groups and combine basic gun safety education with leadership development, vocational training and conflict resolution techniques to give boys and girls real alternatives to lives of violence and fear.

Changing attitudes and then behaviour is always a slow and difficult process, Ms. van de Wiel cautioned, especially for boys. "Boys have a stronger affinity to guns because their older brother or father or village leader has a gun. They're 'cool.'" For that reason, she noted, education about small arms must begin at an early age as part of an overall effort to reduce both the romantic image and the social acceptability of gun use. But the best answer to guns is social and economic progress, she concluded. "Children must have a future that doesn't depend on small arms for survival. Giving them opportunity is the best alternative to violence."

One of the negative aspects of China's increasing engagement with African states is the spread of small arms and/or light weapons especially in conflict zones and were opposition is violently suppressed. These weapons have undoubtably contributed to the enhancement of closer ties between China and authoritarian regimes and served as an instrument for consolidating its presence in the continent. China has developed an extensive presence in Africa through building infrastructure such as airports, roads, hospitals, convention centres, media investment, agricultural and health education, among many other activities that seemingly put China in a good light. At the same time many of China's seemingly worthwhile activities by have not consolidated its ties to the African political elite and incumbent regimes as much as its arms sales to authoritarian regimes have.

Its positive contributions in the continent have been offset by the lure of the benefits that are associated with arms sales to African states despite their negative consequences in growing African states. Chinese small arms have been implicated in ethnic violence and war crimes in Sudan, South Sudan and the Democratic Republic of Congo (DRC) among others. They have also been instrumental in the suppression of democratic progress in Zimbabwe, and at the same time expanding its influence and political economic ties with the authoritarian regime of President Robert Mugabe.

China's worldview which puts social and economic rights over individual liberties and political rights is often quick to supply weapons to authoritarian African states because it does not make human rights observance a condition for arms sales to any country. Incumbent African regimes that face severe threats to their survival are therefore quick to turn to China as a source of arms supply in the struggle to preserve their power.

Apart from the lure of profits for China's arms sales to Africa, there is also the added benefit of China finding employment opportunities for its skilled Chinese citizens. This contributes to spreading its technical and personnel influence in the continent. At times, an arms supply relationship also involves establishing an arms factory in a recipient state that requires the expertise of skilled Chinese scientists, engineers, and industrial managers. Such a relationship for China leads to a long-term business and security relationship with the African country. This is one reason why China's influence in Sudan is so strong. However, what happens is that weapons that are sold by China or produced by China in Africa end up fuelling and feeding the conflicts in countries such as the DRC, Sudan, South Sudan, and the Central African Republic, among others. Regime survival or incumbent regime power consolidation efforts fuel arms transfers in South Sudan and Burundi. Chinese arms are often implicated in these conflicts because of China's aggressive arms sales strategy w is based on the following A "catch all" customers strategy that has established arms transfer or military relationship with several large African states such as Egypt, Nigeria, Ethiopia, Zimbabwe, and South Africa, as well as smaller states like the Republic of Congo, Equatorial Guinea, Eritrea, Burundi, and Sierra Leone, among others; A favourable financing strategy especially for African countries that cannot afford to buy sophisticated weapons and afford to pay the market price for small or light weapons; and China's use of frequent and aggressive small arms marketing of its and more sophisticated military hardware at annual arms exhibits in various states within the continent.

The wide array of Chinese arms enables China to sell weapons to both rich authoritarian African states as well as poorer smaller ones. The Chinese policy of placing no human rights or democracy conditions on arms sales as well its overall policy of non-interference in the politics of African states translates into the availability and affordability of Chinese arms in many African states.

It is not therefore surprising that arms from China have been implicated in the Ethiopian-Eritrean conflict in which China is known to have supplied arms to both sides in the conflict. It is also well documented that Chinese weapons were used in Sudan's suppression of rebels in Darfur following a revolt in 2003 which led to a genocide against the region's people. It is alleged that the light weapons used in the massacres in eastern DRC were of Chinese origin. There, children as young as 11 years old were given weapons by warlord Thomas Lubanga and forced to participate in interethnic killings in the early 2000s. Furthermore, Chinese trained Congolese troops have been implicated on several occasions in ethnic killings of innocent civilians in the eastern DRC. Similarly, in 2009 Chinese-trained Guinean Commando units were responsible for the killings of about 150 people during a protest against authoritarian and undemocratic rule in the country.

According to the Stockholm International Peace Research Institute (SIPRI) report of 2010, China was found to be the foremost exporter of arms to Africa. The Chinese Type 56 which is China's version of the Russian Kalashnikov (AK47) assault rifle is much easier to use as a light weapon. The argument could be made that despite China's claim that it does not interfere in the internal affairs of other countries, the fact that it supplies weapons to warring factions within a sovereign nation is itself inherently interventionist by nature. Such interference produces consequences such as gross human rights violations, murder, rapes, tortures, and extra-judicial killings. China's arms sales to Africa attract negative attention especially because they are made available to states like Sudan and Zimbabwe and the DRC, known for blatant human rights violations in Africa.

This often means that China is reaping the profits of selling weapons to both incumbent regimes and rebel groups. The general outcome is the consolidation and expansion of its ties and presence in the continent. China's propensity to spread small arms and light weapons (SALW) among African states will end up undermining whatever positive perception it has generated in the continent as well as taint its goals to support sustainable development and contribute to the national development goals of individual African states. In particular, it will cast doubt on its willingness to support Millennium Development Goals, and other specific development goals in the continent such as the Program for Infrastructure Development in Africa and similar such programs.

So far, China's military to military ties with African states has been a source of frustration for the United Nations. While it China contributes to peacekeeping efforts in the continent, the United Nations does not know details of its military engagement, or specific military ties, with the countries in which its peacekeepers are deployed such has the DRC, South Sudan, Liberia, Mali, among others. In other words, the expanding military ties with African states, and perhaps the access by rebels to Chinese arms are factors that are likely to undermine UN peacekeeping functions of disarmament of ex-combatants. It is difficult to know whether Chinese arms complement or undermine the efforts to enhance security in fragile African states. It is a question of whether China is willing to ensure that its military ties with countries of concern such as the DRC, Sudan, South Sudan, and Zimbabwe, complement peacekeeping activities there or help to promote peace, stability, democracy and development.

Human rights organizations have often called attention to the destabilizing role that Chinese arms play in conflict zones in Africa. China so far seems determined to support and forge closer ties with authoritarian regimes in their goals of power consolidation, oppression of the opposition. China on the other hand is preoccupied with spreading its influence, consolidating its ties and deepening its engagement with every African state regardless of whether it is democratic or authoritarian. Accordingly, Chinese SALWs are supplied to both national armies in Africa as well as to rebel groups in the DRC, Chad and Uganda, and now the warring factions in South Sudan. China's supply of arms to both rebels and national armies is often a violation of embargoes as well as a blatant case of economic self-interested behaviour. The glimmer of hope in all this is that China has at times bowed to international pressure to cease supplying weapons in areas of gross human rights violations such as was the case with Darfur.

But overall China still gives priority to concern over sovereignty and often defers to incumbent regimes such that human rights observance and non-proliferation of SALWs are relegated a secondary role in China's foreign policy rights towards Africa states. Thanks to Earl Conteh-Morgan is Professor of International Studies in the School of Interdisciplinary Global Studies at the University of South Florida, Tampa, Florida for this report on the wars in Africa.

The head of the African Union has expressed concern over the flow of weapons into Libya after France revealed it had dropped arms into rebel-held areas of the conflict-stricken country earlier this month which led to the toppling of Gaddaffi. AU Commissioner Jean Ping, who chairs a meeting of African leaders in Malabo, Equatorial Guinea, on Thursday, said that weapons distributed in Libya would contribute to the "destabilisation" of African states.

"What worries us is not who is giving what, but simply that weapons are being distributed by all parties and to all parties. We already have proof that these weapons are in the hands of al-Qaeda, of traffickers," said Ping. Colonel Thierry Burkhard, a spokesperson for the French general staff, told Al Jazeera that the military had dropped assault rifles, machine guns and rocket-propelled grenade launchers to groups of unarmed civilians in western Libya it deemed to be at risk.

Earlier in the day, the Le Figaro newspaper and the AFP news agency reported that France had dropped several tonnes of arms, including Milan anti-tank rockets and light armoured vehicles. The airdrops arrived somewhere in rebel-held towns in the Nafusa mountains, which run east-west from the Tunisian border around 100km south of the capital Tripoli. Rebels control most of the Nafusa, up to the town of Yafran, while regime forces loyal to Libyan leader Muammar Gaddafi still hold Gharyan, a key town that lies astride the north-south road to the capital.

NATO Secretary General Anders Fogh Rasmussen said on that the military alliance was not involved in the French airdrop operation. Asked whether he knew of any other countries who were supplying weapons to rebel-held regions, Rasmussen said he had "no information". UN resolution mandate On, a coalition of countries launched a military intervention in Libya under the mandate of a United Nations Security Council resolution aimed at protecting civilians from the onslaught launched by Gaddafi after mass protests broke out against his rule in mid-February. The Security Council resolution established a no-fly zone, asset freeze and arms embargo on Libya and various regime entities. The terms of the NATO-led mission in Libya have provoked controversy for months. The UN resolution 1973 authorising action says the NATO operation is to protect civilians, but France's admission raises major questions about how far that mandate goes.

Part of the UN resolution allows NATO the legal ability to provide weapons for protection or defence, but if those weapons are then used for attack, the rebels and those arming them could be criminally liable.

Donald Rothwell, a professor of international law at the Australian National University, told Al Jazeera that France's arms-supplying operations might arguably fall within the mandate. "I think one of the key issues are whether the weapons supplied by the French are defensive weapons, or whether they're supplied with offensive use in mind," he said. A French military spokesperson said France had become aware in early June that rebel-held villages had come under pressure from loyalist forces. "We began by dropping humanitarian aid: food, water and medical supplies," he told the AFP news agency.

"During the operation, the situation for the civilians on the ground worsened. We dropped arms and means of self-defence, mainly ammunition." Burkhard described the arms as "light infantry weapons of the rifle type" and said the drops were carried out over several days "so that civilians would not be massacred".

Though Burkhard framed the French weapons supplies as a method of protecting civilians in accordance with the UN mandate, it was still unclear whether such air drops violated the arms embargo. NATO countries involved in the operations say their strikes on Gaddafi's armour, anti-aircraft emplacements and command bunkers are only meant to protect civilians. They have denied trying to kill Gaddafi, though US Admiral Samuel Locklear, a NATO commander in Naples, Italy, reportedly told a visiting US congressman in May that they were actively targeting and trying to kill him.

According to Le Figaro, which said it had seen a secret intelligence memo and talked to well-placed officials, the drops were designed to help rebel fighters encircle Tripoli and encourage a popular revolt in the city itself. "If the rebels can get to the outskirts of Tripoli, the capital will take the chance to rise against Gaddafi," said an official quoted in the report. "The regime's mercenaries are no longer getting paid and are scarcely getting fed. There's a severe fuel shortage, the population has had enough." France has taken a leading role in organising international support for the uprising against Gaddafi's four-decade-old rule, and French and British jets are spearheading a NATO-led air campaign targeting his forces.

Rebel forces where mainly based in Benghazi in the east of the country, and held a besieged enclave supplied by sea in the western coastal town of Misurata, but had been unable to mount a convincing advance on the capital.

At the end of President Barack Obama's inauguration ceremony, civil rights leader Rev. Joseph Lowery invoked the hope of a day "when nation shall not lift up sword against nation, when tanks will be beaten into tractors." No one expects such a utopian vision to materialize any time soon. But both Obama and Secretary of State Hillary Clinton have spoken eloquently of the need to emphasize diplomacy over a narrow military agenda. In her confirmation hearing, Clinton stressed the need for "smart power," perhaps inadvertently echoing Obama's opposition to the invasion of Iraq as a "dumb war." Even top U.S. military officials, such as chairman of the Joint Chiefs of Staff Adm. Mike Mullen, have warned against overly militarizing U.S. foreign policy.

In practice, such a shift in emphasis is certain to be inconsistent. At a global level, the most immediate challenge to the credibility of change in foreign policy is Afghanistan, where promised troop increases are given little chance of bringing stability and the country risks becoming Obama's "Vietnam." Africa policy is for the most part under the radar of public debate. But it also poses a clear choice for the new administration. Will de facto U.S. security policy toward the continent focus on anti-terrorism and access to natural resources and prioritize bilateral military relations with African countries? Or will the United States give priority to enhancing multilateral capacity to respond to Africa's own urgent security needs?

If the first option is taken, it will undermine rather than advance both U.S. and African security. Taking the second option won't be easy. There are no quick fixes. But U.S. security in fact requires that policymakers take a broader view of Africa's security needs and a multilateral approach to addressing them. The need for immediate action to promote peace in Africa is clear. While much of the continent is at peace, there are large areas of great violence and insecurity, most prominently centered on Sudan, the Democratic Republic of the Congo, and Somalia. These crises require not only a continuing emphasis on diplomacy but also resources for peacemaking and peacekeeping. And yet the Bush administration has bequeathed the new president a new military command for Africa (the United States Africa Command, known as AFRICOM).

Meanwhile, Washington has starved the United Nations and other multilateral institutions of resources, even while entrusting them with enormous peacekeeping responsibilities. The government has presented AFRICOM as a cost-effective institutional restructuring and a benign program for supporting African governments in humanitarian as well as necessary security operations. In fact, it represents the institutionalization and increased funding for a model of bilateral military ties a replay of the mistakes of the Cold War. This risks drawing the United States more deeply into conflicts, reinforcing links with repressive regimes, excusing human rights abuses, and frustrating rather than fostering sustainable multilateral peacemaking and peacekeeping. It will divert scarce budget resources, build resentment, and undercut the long-term interests of the United States.

Shaping a new U.S. security policy toward Africa requires more than just a modest tilt toward more active diplomacy. It also requires questioning this inherited security framework and shaping an alternative framework that aligns U.S. and African security interests within a broader perspective of inclusive human security. In particular, it requires that the United States shift from a primarily bilateral and increasingly military approach to one that prioritizes joint action with both African and global partners.

Judging by their frequent press releases, AFRICOM and related programs such as the Navy's Africa Partnership Station are primarily focused on a constant round of community relations and capacity building projects, such as rescue and firefighting training for African sailors, construction of clinics and schools, and similar endeavors. "AFRICOM is about helping Africans build greater capacity to assure their own security," asserted Deputy Assistant Secretary of Defense Theresa Whelan in a typical official statement. AFRICOM defenders further cite the importance of integrating development and humanitarian programs into the program's operations.

Pentagon spokespeople describe AFRICOM as a logical bureaucratic restructuring that will ensure that Africa gets the attention it deserves. They insist AFRICOM won't set the priorities for U.S. policy toward Africa or increase Pentagon influence at the expense of civilian agencies. Testifying before the Senate Foreign Relations Committee in August 2007, Whelan denied that AFRICOM was being established "solely to fight terrorism, or to secure oil resources, or to discourage China," countering: "This is not true."

But other statements by Whelan herself, by General William "Kip" Ward, the four-star African-American general who commands AFRICOM, and Vice-Admiral Robert Moeller, his military deputy, lay out AFRICOM's priorities in more conventional terms. In a briefing for European Command officers in March 2004, Whelan said that the Pentagon's priorities in Africa were to "prevent establishment of/disrupt/destroy terrorist groups; stop the spread of weapons of mass destruction; perform evacuations of U.S. citizens in danger; assure access to strategic resources, lines of communication, and refuelling/forward sites" in Africa. On February 19, 2008, Moeller told an AFRICOM conference that protecting "the free flow of natural resources from Africa to the global market" was one of AFRICOM's "guiding principles," citing "oil disruption," "terrorism," and the "growing influence" of China as major "challenges" to U.S. interests in Africa. Appearing before the House Armed Services Committee on March 13, 2008, General Ward echoed the same views and identified combating terrorism as "AFRICOM's number one theatre-wide goal." Ward barely mentioned development, humanitarian aid, or conflict resolution. U.S. official discourse on AFRICOM doesn't engage with the parallel discussions in the United Nations and the African Union about building multilateral peacekeeping capacity. Strikingly, there was no official consultation about the new command with either the United Nations or the African Union before it was first announced in 2006.

In practice, AFRICOM, which became a fully independent combatant command on October 1, 2008, with its headquarters in Stuttgart, Germany, is built on the paradigm of U.S. military commands which span the globe. Although AFRICOM features less "kinetic" (combat) operations than the active wars falling under CENTCOM in Iraq and Afghanistan, its goals and programs are more conventional than the public relations image would imply.

The Pentagon now has six geographically focused commands each headed by either a four-star general or admiral Africa (AFRICOM); the Middle East and Central Asia (Central Command or CENTCOM); Europe and most of the former Soviet Union (European Command or EUCOM); the Pacific Ocean, East and South Asia (Pacific Command or PACOM); Mexico, Canada, and the United States (Northern Command or NORTHCOM); and Central and South America (Southern Command or SOUTHCOM), as well as others with functional responsibilities, such as for Special Forces and Nuclear Weapons.

Before AFRICOM was established, U.S. military operations in Africa fell under three different commands. EUCOM handled most of Africa; but Egypt and the Horn of Africa fell under the authority of CENTCOM (Egypt remains under CENTCOM rather than AFRICOM); Madagascar and the island states of the Indian Ocean were the responsibility of PACOM. All three were primarily concerned with other regions of the world that took priority over Africa and had only a few middle-rank staff members dedicated to Africa. This reflected the fact that Africa was chiefly viewed as a regional theatre in the global Cold War, as an adjunct to U.S. European relations, or in the immediate post-Cold War period as a region of little concern to the United States. But Africa's status in U.S. national security policy and military affairs rose dramatically during the Bush administration, in response both to global terrorism and the growing significance of African oil resources.

The new strategic framework for Africa emphasizes, above all, the threat of global terrorism and the risk posed by weak states, "empty spaces," and countries with large Muslim populations as vulnerable territories where terrorists may find safe haven and political support. This framework is fundamentally flawed. No one denies that al-Qaeda has found adherents and allied groups in Africa, as evidenced most dramatically by the bombings of U.S. embassies in Nairobi and Dar es Salaam in 1998. But Islamist ideology has had only limited impact among most African Muslims, and even in countries with extremist Islamist governments or insurgent groups such as Algeria, Sudan, and Somalia, the focus has been on local issues rather than global conflict. Counterinsurgency analysts such as Robert Berschinski and David Kilcullen have warned that "aggregating" disparate local insurgencies into an all-encompassing vision of global terrorism in fact facilitates al-Qaeda's efforts to woo such groups.

Heavy-handed military action such as air strikes that kill civilians and collaboration with counter-insurgency efforts by incumbent regimes, far from diminishing the threat of terrorism, helps it grow. While AFRICOM may be new, there's already a track record for such policies in programs now incorporated into AFRICOM. That record shows little evidence that these policies contribute to U.S. or African security. To the contrary, there are substantial indications that they are in fact counterproductive, both increasing insecurity in Africa and energizing potential threats to U.S. interests.

The most prominent example of active U.S. military involvement in Africa has been the Combined Joint Task Force-Horn of Africa (CJTF-HOA). Speaking not for attribution at a conference in early 2008, a senior AFRICOM official cited this task force, which has taken the lead in U.S. engagement with Somalia, as a model for AFRICOM's operations elsewhere on the continent. In October 2002, CENTCOM played the leading role in the creation of this joint task force, designed to conduct naval and aerial patrols in the Red Sea, the Gulf of Aden, and the eastern Indian Ocean, in order to counter the activities of terrorist groups in the region. The command authority for CJTF-HOA was transferred to AFRICOM as of October 1, 2008.

Based since 2002 at Camp Lemonier in Djibouti, the CJTF-HOA is comprised of approximate 1,400 U.S. military personnel primarily sailors, Marines, and Special Forces troops. Under a new five-year agreement signed in 2007, the base has expanded to some 500 acres. In addition, the CJTF-HOA has established three permanent contingency operating locations that have been used to mount attacks on Somalia, one at the Kenyan naval base at Manda Bay and two others at Hurso and Bilate in Ethiopia. A U.S. Navy Special Warfare Task Unit was recently deployed to Manda Bay, where it is providing training to Kenyan troops in anti-terrorism operations and coastal patrol missions.

The CJTF-HOA provided intelligence to Ethiopia in support of its invasion of Somalia in December 2006. It also used military facilities in Djibouti, Ethiopia, and Kenya to launch air raids and missile strikes in January and June of 2007 and May of 2008 against alleged al-Qaeda members involved in the Union of Islamic Courts in Somalia. At least dozens of Somali civilians were killed in this series of air attacks alone, and hundreds wounded. These were only a fraction of the toll of the fighting during the invasion, in which hundreds of civilians were killed and over 300,000 people displaced by mid-2007.

By the end of 2008, over 3.2 million people (43% of Somalia's population), including 1.3 million internally displaced by conflict, were estimated to be in need of food assistance. The U.S. air strikes made U.S. backing for the invasion highly visible. These military actions, moreover, represented only part of a broader counterproductive strategy shaped by narrow counterterrorism considerations. In 2005 and 2006, the CIA funnelled resources to selected Somali warlords to oppose Islamist militia.

The United States collaborated with Ethiopia in its invasion of Somalia in late 2006, overthrowing the Islamic Courts Union that had brought several months of unprecedented stability to the capital Mogadishu and its surroundings. The invasion was a conventional military success. But far from reducing the threat from extremist groups, it isolated moderates, provoked internal displacement that became one of the world's worst humanitarian crises, inflamed anti-U.S. sentiment, and even provoked the targeting of both local and international humanitarian operations.

In short, Somalia provided a textbook case of the negative results of "aggregating" local threats into an undifferentiated concept of global terrorism. It has left the new Obama administration with what Ken Menkhaus, a leading academic expert on Somalia, called "a policy nightmare."

Less in the news, but also disturbing because of the wide range of countries involved in both North and West Africa, is the U.S. military involvement in the Sahara and Sahel region, now under AFRICOM. Operation Enduring Freedom Trans Sahara (OEF-TS) provides military support to the Trans-Sahara Counter Terrorism Partnership (TSCTP) program, which comprises the United States and eleven African countries: Algeria, Burkina Faso, Libya, Morocco, Tunisia, Chad, Mali, Mauritania, Niger, Nigeria, and Senegal. Its goals are defined on the AFRICOM web site as "to assist traditionally moderate Muslim governments and populations in the Trans-Sahara region to combat the spread of extremist ideology and terrorism in the region." It builds on the former Pan Sahel Initiative, which was operational from 2002 to 2004, and draws on resources from the Department of State and USAID as well as the Department of Defense. Operational support comes from another task force, Joint Task Force Aztec Silence (JTFAS), created in December 2003 under EUCOM. JTFAS was specifically charged with conducting surveillance operations using the assets of the U.S. Sixth Fleet and to share information, along with intelligence collected by U.S. intelligence agencies, with local military forces.

Among other assets, it deploys a squadron of U.S. Navy P-3 Orion maritime patrol aircraft based in Sigonella, Sicily. In March 2004, P-3 aircraft from this squadron and reportedly operating from the southern Algerian base at Tamanrasset were deployed to monitor and gather intelligence on the movements of Algerian Salafist guerrillas operating in Chad and to pass on this intelligence to Chadian forces engaged in combat against the guerrillas.

In September 2007, an American C-130 "Hercules" cargo plane stationed in Bamako, the capital of Mali, as part of the Flintlock 2007 exercises, was deployed to resupply Malian counter-insurgency units engaged in fighting with Tuareg forces and was hit by Tuareg ground fire. No U.S. personnel were injured, and the plane returned safely to the capital, but the incident signalled a significant extension of the U.S. role in counter-insurgency warfare in the region.

These operations illustrate how strengthening counterinsurgency capacity proves either counterproductive or irrelevant as a response to African security issues, which may include real links to global terrorist networks but are for the most part focused on specific national and local realities. On an international scale, the impact of violent Islamic extremism in North Africa has direct implications in Europe, but its bases are urban communities and the North African Diaspora in Europe, rather than the Sahara-Sahel hinterland. Insurgencies along the Sahara-Sahel divide, in Mali, Niger, and Chad, reflect ethnic and regional realities rather than extensions of global terrorism. The militarily powerful North African regimes, Morocco, Algeria, Tunisia, and Libya, have very distinct experiences with Islamic extremism. But none have a record of stability based on democratic accountability to civil society. And associating all threats to security in Nigeria with the threat of extremist Islam is a bizarre stereotype ignoring that country's real problems.

In his November 2007 paper on AFRICOM, cited above, Berschinski noted that the United States and Algeria exaggerated the threat from the small rebel group GSPC (Salafist Group for Preaching and Combat), officially allied with al-Qaeda. A scary, if geographically inappropriate, headline in Air Force Magazine in November 2004, heralded the threat from a "Swamp of Terror in the Sahara." The emphasis on counterinsurgency, Berschinski argues, has disrupted traditional trade networks and allowed local governments to neglect the need for finding negotiated solutions to concerns of Tuareg areas and other neglected regions.

In the case of Mali, Robert Pringle a former U.S. ambassador to that country has noted that the U.S. emphasis on anti-terrorism and radical Islam is out of touch with both the country's history and Malian perceptions of current threats to their own security. The specifics of each country differ, but the common reality is that the benefits of U.S. collaboration with local militaries in building counterinsurgency capacity haven't been demonstrated.

Cases to the contrary, however, aren't hard to find. In Mauritania, General Mohamed Ould Abdelaziz overthrew the elected government in August 2008, leading to sanctions from the African Union and suspension of all but humanitarian aid from France and the United States. U.S. aid to Mauritania for the 2008 fiscal year that was suspended included $15 million in military-to-military funding, as well as $4 million for peacekeeping training and only $3 million in development assistance. More generally, the common argument that U.S. military aid promotes values of respect for democracy is decisively contradicted by what resulted in Latin America from decades of U.S. training of the region's military officers. If democratic institutions are not already strong, strengthening military forces is most likely to increase the chances of military interventions in politics.

Potential Threats with at least a temporary withdrawal of Ethiopian troops and the election of moderate Islamic leader Sheikh Sharif Ahmed as president of the transitional Somali government, there is at least the option of a new beginning in that country. But no one expects any quick solution, with all parties internally divided including the insurgent militia known as Al-Shabaab and international peace efforts distracted by multiple agendas. There will be a continuing temptation to continue a narrow anti-terrorist agenda, even if this path is now more widely recognized as self-defeating.

In the region covered by Operation Enduring Freedom Trans Sahara, the conflict in Chad, where the World Bank abandoned efforts to ensure accountability for oil revenues, is still intimately tied with the larger conflict in Darfur to the east, as well as with the legacy of Libyan intervention. Although the United States has deferred to France in active military and political involvement in Chad, it has also supported President Idriss Deby, who has been in power since 1991 and changed the constitution in 2005 to allow himself another term. Despite attacks by rebels on the capital in February 2008, Deby retained control with French military assistance.

In northern Niger, uranium resources threaten to provide new incentives for the conflict with the Tuareg minority reignited there and in Mali since 2007. Mali is generally seen as one of West Africa's most successful democracies, but it's also threatened by Tuareg discontent which requires a diplomatic rather than military solution.

Of particular strategic importance for the future is Nigeria, where U.S. military concerns of anti-terrorism and energy security converge. As Nigeria specialists Paul Lubeck, Michael Watts, and Ronnie Lipschutz outline in a 2007 policy study, the threat to Nigeria from Islamic extremism is wildly exaggerated in statements by U.S. military officials. In contrast, they note, "nobody doubts the strategic significance of contemporary Nigeria for West Africa, for the African continent as a whole, and for the oil-thirsty American economy." But the solution to the growing insurgency in the oil-rich Niger Delta isn't a buildup of U.S. naval forces and support for counter-insurgency actions by the Nigerian military. The priority is rather to resolve the problems of poverty, environmental destruction, and to promote responsible use of the country's oil wealth, particularly for the people of the oil-producing regions.

Currently, U.S. military ties with Nigeria and other oil-producing states of West and Central Africa include not only bilateral military assistance, but also the naval operations of the Africa Partnership Station and other initiatives to promote maritime safety, particularly for the movement of oil supplies. In recent years, United States military aid to Nigeria has included at least four coastal patrol ships to Nigeria, and approximately $2 million a year in other funds, including for development of a small boat unit in the Niger Delta. According to the State Department's budget request justification for the 2007 fiscal year, military aid to the country is needed because "Nigeria is the fifth largest source of U.S. oil imports, and disruption of supply from Nigeria would represent a major blow to U.S. oil security strategy." In fact, maritime security is a legitimate area for concern for both African nations and importers of West African oil. Piracy for purely monetary motives, as well as the insurgency in the Niger Delta, is a real and growing threat off the West African coast. Yet strengthening the military capacity of Nigeria and other oil-producing states, without dealing with the fundamental issues of democracy and distribution of wealth, won't lead to security for African people or for U.S. interests, including oil supplies. Likewise, a military solution can't resolve the issue of piracy in the Indian Ocean and Red Sea.

The threats cited by U.S. officials to justify AFRICOM aren't imaginary. Global terrorist networks do seek allies and recruits throughout the African continent, with potential impact in the Middle East, Europe, and even North America as well as in Africa. In the Niger Delta, the production of oil has been repeatedly interrupted by attacks by militants of the Movement for the Emancipation of the Niger Delta (MEND).

More broadly, insecurity creates an environment vulnerable to piracy and to the drug trade, as well as to motivating potential recruits to extremist political violence. It doesn't follow, however, that such threats can be effectively countered by increased U.S. military engagement, even if the direct involvement of U.S. troops is minimized. The focus on building counter-insurgency capacity for African governments with U.S. assistance diverts attention from more fundamental issues of conflict resolution. It also heightens the risks of increasing conflict and concomitantly increasing hostility to the United States.

Continuity or Change. Will that the Obama administration could have seriously re-examined their Africa policy it has inherited from its predecessors? Or will continuity be the watchword? The few indications we have so far, from campaign statements and Obama's choice of top officials, point to continuity. Yet the critical tests will be in practice, as African crises force their way onto the agenda even while the administration's energies are primarily focused on more prominent domestic and international challenges.

Patterns from the Past during his presidential bid, Senator Barack Obama's statements signalled continuity with Bush administration policies on Africa, including security issues. Paralleling his prominent remarks on Afghanistan, the candidate's reply to a questionnaire from the Leon Sullivan Foundation in September 2007 noted that "there will be situations that require the United States to work with its partners in Africa to fight terrorism with lethal force," leaving open the door for attacks on Somalia. In an article written for All Africa.com in September 2008, Witney Schneidman, deputy assistant secretary of state for African affairs in the Clinton administration and adviser on Africa to the Obama campaign, said the new administration "will create a Shared Partnership Program to build the infrastructure to deliver effective counter-terrorism training, and to create a strong foundation for coordinated action against al-Qaeda and its affiliates in Africa and elsewhere."

He added that the program "will provide assistance with information sharing, operations, border security, anti-corruption programs, technology, and the targeting of terrorist financing." Schneidman further argued that "in the Niger Delta, we should become more engaged not only in maritime security, but in working with the Nigerian government, the European Union, the African Union, and other stakeholders to stabilize the region."

Even more significant a signal was Obama's choice of General James Jones (Ret.) as his national security advisor. As commander of NATO and EUCOM from 2003 through 2006, General Jones was an enthusiastic advocate of AFRICOM. U.S. Ambassador to the United Nations Susan Rice, who is well-placed to be an advocate for multilateral approaches to peace in Africa, is nevertheless on record as having endorsed Bush administration air strikes on Somalia at the time of the Ethiopian invasion. And she has been a prominent advocate of direct bilateral U.S. military action in Darfur.

On February 9, 2009, Acting Assistant Secretary of State Phil Carter, speaking at the Pentagon's Africa Center for Strategic Studies, opened his remarks with the claim that "the one foreign policy success of the previous administration is Africa." He outlined four priorities, beginning with "providing security assistance programs" to African partners, followed by promoting "democratic systems and practices," "sustainable and broad-based market-led economic growth," and "health and social development." Although he prefaced his list of priorities with a reference to support for ending conflict in Africa and "African solutions to African problems," it's telling that the description of the security priority includes military capacity-building and AFRICOM operations, but no mention at all of diplomacy.

Such indications do not give great confidence in any major shift in security strategy. Nevertheless, there are also signals that U.S. officials, including some in the military and intelligence community, do recognize the need to give greater emphasis to diplomacy and development. The initial U.S. welcome to the election of moderate Islamist Sheikh Sharif Ahmed as president of Somalia is potentially an indicator of a new approach to that complex crisis. Incoming Director of National Intelligence Dennis Blair told the Senate in his first annual threat assessment that "the primary near-term security concern of the United States is the global economic crisis." Blair's survey covered traditional security threats, including "extremist groups using terrorism," but also stressed the need for the United States to not only deal with "regions, regimes, and crises" but also participate in developing new multilateral systems. Changing Priorities for Africa in particular, realities call for a different ordering of priorities, recognizing the significance of less conventional threats and the inadequacy of narrow military responses. In a report TransAfrica Forum called for a new policy framework based on "inclusive human security."

Such a framework would require fundamental shifts in thinking, stressing multilateral cooperation over unilateral initiatives, a broad range of threats than only those from violent enemies, and investment in basic economic and social rights over blind trust in the market.

U.S. Africa policy based on such a framework would look very different than that outlined by Assistant Secretary of State Carter as the inheritance from the Bush administration, even if containing many of the same elements. In the economic and development arena, it should build on the example of the response to AIDS, both multilateral and bilateral, to address African needs in health, education, food, economic infrastructure, and the environment, with all countries paying their fair share. The United States should open a genuine dialogue about trade and development policy, instead of imposing rigid free-market policies that are systematically biased in favor of rich countries. And the administration should draw on the insights and contributions of the large community of recent African immigrants to the U. S., many of whom are engaged in family and community projects to help their countries.

Within the arena of traditional security issues, the United States should minimize bilateral military involvement with Africa, which risks sucking the U.S. into local conflicts, in favor of multilateral diplomacy and peacekeeping, including paying U.S. peacekeeping arrears at the UN. It should take care not to aid repressive regimes or to prioritize military-to-military relationships, in favor of dialogue not only with incumbent governments but also civil society. In short, it should shift from an emphasis on counter-insurgency and building Washington-centered networks of influence with African military establishments to an emphasis on U.S. participation in multilateral efforts to enhance African security.

In theory, AFRICOM's activities, as well as related peacekeeping training programs administered by the Department of State, should be integrated within overall U.S. policy, including diplomatic action on African crises and collaboration with African, European, and United Nations partners in peacekeeping operations. In practice, as the Henry L. Stimson Center's Victoria Holt and Michael McKinnon have said, the United States has been ambivalent about multilateral action, under both the Clinton and Bush administrations. Democrats and Republicans alike have approved and supported United Nations and African Union peacekeeping missions.

But the United States is still regularly from $700 million to $1.5 billion in arrears on peacekeeping dues owed the United Nations. And it failed to respond even to urgent requests for essential logistical support, such as helicopters for the mission in Darfur. Coordination of diplomacy with support for peacekeeping has been weak even within the U.S. government, while the U.S. military remains opposed to U.S. participation in multilateral operations that are not commanded by U.S. officers.

The most innovative U.S. program to support multilateral peacekeeping has been Africa Contingency Operations and Assistance (ACOTA), administered by the State Department, and part of the Global Peace Operations Initiative (GPOI) decided by G8 leaders in 2004. This program has trained some 45,000 African peacekeepers since 2004, with a training package and "train-the-trainer" components that are said to be based on UN standards. Yet there is no evidence that this program is integrated into a broader strategy of U.S. diplomatic priorities in Africa or capacity building in collaboration with the United Nations. As a bilateral training program under exclusive U.S. management, when the United States is also engaged in bilateral counter-insurgency training and operations with many of the same countries, it inevitably raises questions about the real priorities in military-to-military relationships.

The United States does have resources, particularly logistical and financial, that are relevant for peacekeeping operations, and has the responsibility to make its fair contribution as a leading member of the international community. But ensuring that these actually contribute to peace requires a new framework, giving priority to multilateral diplomacy and peacekeeping over bilateral programs.

Elements of a New Security framework the need for moving to a new framework isn't a matter of finding new formulas to replace the inherited emphasis on building counter-insurgency capacity against terrorism and threats to natural resources. There's no one prescription for those countries now facing violent conflicts, much less for the wide range of issues faced by over 50 African countries. Africa's serious problems, moreover, will not be solved from outside, either by the United States or by the "international community."

Nevertheless, it's important to ensure that U.S. Africa policy does no harm and that the United States makes a significant contribution to diminishing the real security threats on the continent. Once one recognizes that U.S. national security also depends on the human security of Africans, some essential elements of such a framework do become clear. To what extent they can be embodied into practice will depend not only on the internal deliberations of the new administration in Washington, but also on whether Africans working for peace and justice on the continent can themselves chart new directions and make their voices heard.

Prioritize long-term inclusive human security. At a global level, National Intelligence Director Blair's threat assessment echoed the growing recognition that economic, environmental, and other "non-military" threats can only be ignored at our peril. The implications for Africa policy should be clear. The optimistic assumption that developing regions could be "delinked" from the global economic crisis has quickly been abandoned. While there may be no direct link between hardships deriving from economic, health, and environmental threats and the threats of violent conflict, ignoring such broader threats is a sure recipe for disaster. Investment in sustainable development, preserving the environment, democratic accountability, and broad access to basic rights to health, education, and housing between and within countries is not charity. It's only prudent. And solutions in Africa and in the United States are interconnected. Take an example from only one sector: energy and global warming. The development of alternative energy sources in the United State can reduce the demand for oil, thus reducing the presumed need to support oil-producing regimes regardless of their human rights records. It's also essential to slow global warming, which is already having severe consequences for the environment in Africa, even though Africa produces only a small fraction of world's greenhouse gases.

At the same time, the United States should support efforts to make both oil companies and governments accountable for the use of oil revenue, investing it both to benefit their citizens and to foster development sectors not so vulnerable to the boom and bust of the oil economy. None of these measures are easy, of course. Nor are they a substitute for resolving open conflict in critical oil-producing regions such as the Niger Delta in Nigeria. But the fact is no other approach has a chance of being sustainable. Prioritizing counter-insurgency provides no short-cut. In such a context, providing U.S. military assistance is only to add fuel to the flames.

More generally, U.S. policy toward each region of the continent including strategic countries such as South Africa, Nigeria, Algeria, Egypt, Ethiopia, Kenya, and the Democratic Republic of the Congo must feature cooperation and dialogue on a wide range of issues affecting human security rather than prioritizing military-to-military relationships. As noted below, it is critical to foster new opportunities for both societies and governments to dialogue about solutions to common problems of human security. Pay Attention to Crises but Avoid "One-Size Fits All" Approaches.

Governments don't have the luxury, however, of paying attention only to long-term structural issues. Immediate crises demand responses. Violent conflicts or failed states have consequences not only for the lives lost and the countries directly involved, but also for surrounding regions and for the continent as a whole. The costs of humanitarian response from the international community multiply in proportion to the delays in acting. And, as the surge of piracy in the Indian Ocean and the Gulf of Guinea has recently reminded the world, the consequences are economic as well as humanitarian. Within conflict zones, personal and collective investments in health, education, and infrastructure can be wiped out in a matter of months.

The list of Africa's hottest crises is familiar: Sudan (including but not limited to Darfur), Somalia, the Democratic Republic of the Congo, and Zimbabwe. Others fester as well, out of the spotlight of the world's media: Chad, Côte d'Ivoire, and Uganda, to name only a few. In each case, it's not only the countries and their immediate neighbors that are involved. Other stakeholders, including regional African organizations, the African Union, the United Nations, and global powers such as the United States are called on to respond. And the responses or failures to respond matter.

But no "one-size-fits-all" response can possibly make sense, and certainly not the AFRICOM model focused on building counter-insurgency capacity for Africa's armies. In shaping the mix of diplomacy, pressures, humanitarian, and peacekeeping actions that have the best chances for success in any particular case, a unilateral U.S. approach is sure to be ineffective or counterproductive. But simply advocating "African solutions for African problems" is a rhetorical gimmick rather than a real alternative.

African political leaders must be part of the solution, and, with very few exceptions, diplomacy must engage all parties to a conflict, including those most guilty of aggression or human rights abuses. But those states closest to the crises, and prominent in regional organizations, also have their own interests. Even when there is consensus, such as with the creation of the African Union mission to Darfur, the resources may be lacking, setting up such a solution for failure in advance.

And while the institutional capacity of the African Union for peacemaking is growing, like the United Nations its effectiveness depends on member states and on the political compromises among its leaders. But the time has long passed for anyone to take current African heads of state as the only spokespeople for the continent, or to focus hopes for change on replacing one leader with another. Finding the best way forward in responding to crises or to Africa's structural problems, must go beyond the top. Africa's resources for change and for leadership are also found in civil society, among respected retired leaders and other elders, and among professionals working both in governments and in multilateral organizations, including both diplomats and military professionals.

The challenge for U.S. policy is to engage actively and productively in responding to crises, bringing U.S. resources to bear without assuming that it is either possible or wise for the United States to dominate. Building an Institutional Capacity for Multilateral Peacemaking and Peacekeeping. In contrast to the emphasis on building bilateral U.S. military ties with Africa, being institutionalized in AFRICOM, U.S. security policy toward Africa should instead concentrate on building institutional capacity within the United Nations, as well as coordinating U.S. relationships with African regional institutions with United Nations capacity-building programs. At the same time, it should work to ensure that both U.S. and United Nations policies and operations with respect to African crises are transparent and open to review by legislative bodies and civil society groups in Africa, in the United States, and in other countries that are involved.

This proposal for a new direction isn't based on any assumption that the United Nations has the answer to Africa's crises. On the contrary. In a statement on February 23, Under-Secretary-General for Peacekeeping Operations, Alain Le Roy, told the Security Council that the organization's peacekeeping efforts are overstretched and in several cases at risk of "mission failure."

Missions in the Democratic Republic of the Congo and in Sudan have mandates that far exceed their capacity, and the Security Council has just voted two new mandates for forces in Chad and in Somalia.

"We face operational overstretch and, I would argue, political overstretch too," he added. "There is a constant strain now between mandates and resources, between expectations and our capacity to deliver."

Nevertheless, even governments as congenitally opposed to multilateralism as the outgoing Bush administration have found United Nations peacekeeping to be an essential resource. UN actions will always be dependent on the willingness of member governments to cooperate, and vulnerable to indecision and bureaucratic delay. But it's long past time to strengthen the institution's capacity for peacemaking and peacekeeping. Public opinion around the world, and in the United States, has long favored increased responsibility and resources for the United Nations. Polls in late 2006 in 14 countries in different regions, for example, showed that majorities of 64% favored "having a standing UN peacekeeping force selected, trained, and commanded by the United Nations." In the same poll 72% of U.S. respondents approved this option. While the stereotype persists among U.S. policymakers that the public is skeptical about the United Nations, polls consistently show strong public support, including for payment of dues in full (see Benjamin Page and Marshall Bouton, The Foreign Policy Disconnect, University of Chicago Press, 2006).

Building United Nations peacekeeping capacity implies not only financial resources, of course, but also internal and external oversight to check possibilities for corruption and abuses, just as would be the case for governments in Africa or in the United States. The framework for inclusive human security released by TransAfrica Forum in February, for example, calls for new mechanisms to ensure civil society and legislative input and review of both U.S. government and multilateral agencies. Despite the expectations for change, it is likely that shifts by the Obama administration in security policy toward Africa will only emerge piecemeal, if at all, after appointment of new mid-level personnel and policy reviews reportedly under way in every agency. The new president's popularity and the range of domestic and global problems he faces are likely to give the administration a large window of opportunity before disillusionment sets in. But events on the ground will not allow indefinite delay.

It will soon become apparent, in Somalia, Sudan, the Democratic Republic of the Congo, and perhaps in other crises not now predictable, to what extent African hopes placed in President Obama will find answers in changes that make a difference for Africa.British chocoholics may have unwittingly helped fund an African conflict, with an estimated $120m (£60m) from the cocoa trade being siphoned off into war chests in Ivory Coast, according to a report released today.

"There is a high chance that your chocolate bar contains cocoa from Ivory Coast and may have funded the conflict there, which leaves a bitter taste in the mouth," said Patrick Alley, the director of Global Witness, the London-based group behind the report. Companies such as Nestlé and Mars source some of their cocoa from the troubled west African nation. While much has been written about child labour on African cocoa plantations, the Global Witness report, Hot Chocolate, is the first to catalogue how cocoa has fuelled conflict on the west coast of the continent.

Ivory Coast supplies 40 per cent of global cocoa, making it the number one producer in the world. On the back of this natural resource, the country has built itself up into the so-called "Paris of Africa", with a downtown of gleaming skyscrapers and leafy suburbs where residents can enjoy an exquisite fillet steak washed down with a glass of expensive claret.

But in September 2002, what began as a troop mutiny became a full-scale civil war and the country divided into a rebel-held north and a government-controlled south with UN peacekeepers patrolling a buffer zone in between. Before long Ivorians were fighting with poverty and expatriates and aid workers were scurrying to relocate elsewhere in the region.

Global Witness says that among the many abuses of cocoa revenues during the "no war, no peace" stand-off, about $20m was embezzled by Ivorian national cocoa institutions and diverted to the government. Another $40m were funnelled into the president's war effort. On the rebel side, militants extorted $30m each year from companies trucking cocoa through their half of the country - a illegal tax that "enabled them to survive as a movement", the report says.

Campaigners want the intermediary cocoa-exporting companies to be transparent about exactly what payments they make and want big confectioners to be upfront about where their cocoa comes from.

"The chocolate industry is so secretive about their recipes that they don't tell you what's in the mix," said one of the report's researchers, who has assumed the alias Maria Lopez. "The consumer can pressure chocolate companies to put that information on the label, so they know they are buying conflict-free chocolate."

With most confectioners simply listing "cocoa" on their chocolate bar packaging, it can be tricky for the consumer to make an informed choice. When contacted by The Independent, spokespeople from Mars and Nestlé said their companies sourced cocoa from several countries, including Ivory Coast. A Cadbury spokesman said its cocoa came from Ghana. Campaigners say that with a wobbly peace process just about staying on track in Ivory Coast, there is an opportunity for making changes to the cocoa industry practices.

The Ivorian President, Laurent Gbagbo, and the rebel leader, Guillaume Soro, signed a deal three months ago, mapping out the path to peace that would end with the country being reunified and elections in January 2008. But UN officials have already publicly said that the timetable has slipped behind schedule.

"We really do not know what's going to happen," Ms Lopez said. "There's no guarantee that the peace process will keep moving forward. We have seen it all unravel before."

It is our sincere desire to lay the clear Word of God before you, the truth-seeking reader, so you may decide for yourself what is truth and what is error. If you find herein anything contrary to the Word of God, you need not accept it. But if you desire to seek for Truth as for hidden treasure and find Small arms in Africa. In fact, small arms, which include rifles, pistols and light machine guns, are filling African graves in ever-increasing numbers from the killing fields of Burundi and the Democratic Republic of Congo to the streets of Lagos and Johannesburg. While the international community searches, so far unsuccessfully, for agreement on the regulation of the global trade in small arms, a growing number of African countries, UN agencies and non-governmental organizations are grappling with the human and development consequences of gun violence and seeking to reduce both the supply and the demand for what Kofi Annan has called "the weapons of choice for the killers of our time."

colonial fighters, newly independent states and superpower proxy forces aliReducing the availability and use of small arms in places where fighting has ended has become increasingly important to Africa's development prospects as the number of conflicts has increased over the past decade. The widespread abuse of weapons diverts scarce government resources from health and education to public security, discourages investment and economic growth, and deprives developing countries of the skills and talents of the victims of small arms. Millions of light arms lightweight, highly portable, and devastatingly effective in the hands of even young or poorly trained users were shipped to Africa during the Cold War to equip anti-cke.

The Boer Wars, I've always had a passion for history, and I first started to realise how governments and the media collaborate to manufacture "history" through the study of the Boer War. The Boer War was the first historical incident that I learned was completely different to how the accepted history tells us it was.

The actuality of what happened to provoke that war and who was behind it wasn't hidden very deeply, in fact it was barely hidden at all. Cecil Rhodes provoked it by sending 500 heavily armed British mercenaries into the Boer state The Jameson Raid in order to provoke a rebellion against the Boer government by the British settlers and merchants living there. The Boers surrounded this group well short of its objective, forced its surrender and humiliated Rhodes and the British Government. Rhodes knew that all he had to do to conquer the Boer state was provoke war, that was the reason for sending those 500 men, he knew they would not succeed, but he knew that sending 500 Britishers to start an uprising of Britishers in the Boer states would provoke the Boers into taking some action against its British minority.

Rhodes could then use his cosy relationship with the British press to spin this into Boer attacks on poor innocent British settlers and that would soon have the British public clamouring for its government to send troops to teach these damn Boers a lesson for daring to lay hands on British citizens.The situation I just described fits exactly into the standard model of regime change that we have seen implemented many times since 1945 by the CIA-M16-Mossad (in reality, they largely operate as a single agency). Let me lay it out in its basics send foreign mercenaries into the victim state to foment 'revolt'. Provoke the victim state into using its armed forces to oppose the foreign invaders. Have the media present this lawful defensive action by the victim state as the cruel oppression of a dictatorship. Send your armed forces to complete the job of regime change.

Establish a new puppet regime with a banking system consisting of a privately held central bank that issues currency on a debt basis, thus enslaving the population. It really is that simple, and it has been carried out so many times, currently it is being done in Syria, a couple of years ago we saw an absolutely blatant and textbook case in Libya, before that Iraq and Afghanistan.

PanAfricansim

Pan-Africanist ideals emerged in the late 19th Century in response to the European Colonisation and the exploitation of the African Continent. Pan-Africanist philosophy then was categorised and driven by Slavery and Colonialism which was in-turn been encouraged by the European Royalties of the day in search of green pastures and expansions to their Kingdoms. Europeans who first ventured into Africa were missionaries whom in-turn encouraged other Europeans to come to Africa with their unfounded categorisation of the African race, culture and values as primitive and their presumptions that all Africans needed to be re-educated and cultured according to their values. These destructive beliefs driven by the missionaries gave birth to intensified forms of racism as other Europeans followed in their footsteps this time in search of the African Riches of King Solomon's mines and some land of which all of this was scarcer in Europe.

As broader political concept, Pan-Africanism roots lies in the collective experiences of the African descendants in America and The Caribbean Islands. For the first time the term African which had often been used by racist as a derogatory term, became a source of pride for early nationalist due to two primary reasons one was the increasing futility of African-American campaigns for racial equality in the USA and second it led to some demanding voluntary repatriation to Africa. Black activists in America and the rest of the world began to reclaim their civil rights previously denied by the Europeans and Western Societies then.

Pan-Africanism represents the complexities of the black political and intellectual thoughts of over two hundred years. What constitutes Pan-Africanism movements often changes according to whether the focus is on political, ideology, organisations or culture. Pan-Africanism actually reflects a range of political views. At the basic level, it's a belief that African peoples both on the African continent and in the Diaspora share not merely a common history but a common destiny the Unification of the African Continent. This sense of interconnected past and future has taken many forms as early as in the 1800 when their held the first Pan-Africanist Conference in Chicago which led to a series of them being held in America, London, and Paris with the last one being held in 1945 which was attended by Kwame Nkrumah.

These conferences led to the creation of African political nationalist adapting their stances and taking up arms against the colonist and each then gaining Independence and they in-turn created the Organisation of African Unity (OAU) which is now the African Union(AU). It has also seen the creation of Inter-African Economic activity which can only be strengthened by the creation of a single currency for the African continent.

In 1897, Henry Sylvester-Williams, a West Indian Barrister, formed the African Association in London to encourage Pan-African unity; especially throughout the British colonies. Sylvester-Williams, who had links with West African dignitaries, believed that Africans and those of African descent living in the Diaspora needed a forum to address their common problems. In 1900, Sylvester- Williams organized the first Pan-African meeting in collaboration with several black leaders representing various countries of the African Diaspora. For the first time, opponents of colonialism and racism gathered for an international meeting. The conference, held in London, attracted global attention, placing the word "Pan-African" in the lexicon of international affairs and making it part of the standard vocabulary of black intellectuals.

The initial meeting featured thirty delegates, mainly from England and the West Indies, but attracted only a few Africans and African Americans. Among them was black America's leading intellectual, W. E. B. Du Bois, who was to become the torchbearer of subsequent Pan- African conferences, or congresses as they later came to be called. Conference participants read papers on a variety of topics, including the social, political, and economic conditions of blacks in the Diaspora; the importance of independent nations governed by people of African descent, such as Ethiopia, Haiti, and Liberia; the legacy of slavery and European imperialism; the role of Africa in world history; and the impact of Christianity on the African continent. Perhaps of even greater significance was the formation of two committees. One group, chaired by Du Bois, drafted an address "To the Nations of the World," demanding moderate reforms for colonial Africa. The address implored the United States and the imperial European nations to "acknowledge and protect the rights of people of African descent" and to respect the integrity and independence of "the free Negro States of Abyssinia, Liberia, Haiti, etc." The address, signed by committee chairman Du Bois as well as its president Bishop Alexander Walters, its vice president Henry B. Brown, and its general secretary Sylvester-Williams, was published and sent to Queen Victoria of England.

The second committee planned for the formation of a permanent Pan-African association in London with branches overseas. Despite these ambitious plans, the appeals of conference participants made little or no impression on the European imperial powers who controlled the political and economic destiny of Africa. It was not until after World War I that Du Bois revived the Pan-African congresses. Following the war, European and American politicians gathered for a peace conference in Versailles, France. Du Bois, who attended the conference as a special representative of the National Association for the Advancement of Colored People (NAACP), appealed to President Woodrow Wilson. In a letter to Wilson, he urged the American government to initiate a comprehensive study of the treatment of black soldiers. Moreover, Du Bois expressed hope that the peace treaty would address "the future of Africa" and grant self-determination to the colonized peoples.

President Wilson subsequently released a Fourteen Point memorandum, which suggested the formation a League of Nations and called for "an absolutely impartial adjustment of all colonial claims, based on the principle that the interests of the population must have equal weight with the equitable claims of the government." Although historians have questioned the impact Du Bois's request had on Wilson's Fourteen Point memorandum, it was apparent that the loudest voice on behalf of oppressed blacks in the New World and colonized Africa belonged to the participants of the Pan-African Congress. Galvanized by the gathering of world leaders and the discussion of colonial Africa's future, Du Bois proposed the formation of a Pan-African Congress. In 1919, as the Versailles Peace treaty deliberations ran their course, Du Bois, with the support of Blaise Diagne, a member of the French Parliament from the West African colony of Senegal, and funding from African American civil rights and fraternal organizations such as the NAACP, the Elks, and the Masons, convened a Pan-African Congress in Paris.

The Congress, attended by approximately sixty representatives from sixteen nations, protectorates, and colonies, however, was more "pan" than African since most of the delegates had little, if any, first-hand knowledge of the African continent. Prominent American attendees included black members of the NAACP such as John Hope, president of Morehouse College, and Addie W. Hunton, who had served with black troops in France under the auspices of the Young Men's Christian Association (YMCA), as well as white NAACP members, such as the Columbia University professor Joel Spingarn, the socialist William English Walling, and the socialist muckraking author Charles Edward Russell.

Among the other delegates from the United States were Roscoe Conklin Simmons, a well- known black orator; Rayford W. Logan, who had served with the U.S. Army in France; black women's rights activist Ida Gibbs Hunt; and Dr. George Jackson, a black American missionary in the Congo.

Conference participants adopted a resolution calling for the drafting of a code of law "for the international protection of the natives of Africa." Other demands called for direct supervision of colonies by the League of Nations to prevent economic exploitation by foreign nations; to abolish slavery and capital punishment of colonial subjects who worked on the plantations of European colonial powers in Africa, especially in the Belgian Congo; and to insist on colonial peoples' right to education. Moreover, the gathering stressed the need for further congress meetings and suggested the creation of an international quarterly, the Black Review, which was to be published in several languages. 'While congress attendees insisted that African natives should be allowed eventually to participate in their own government, they did not demand African self-determination. Despite the moderate nature of the demands, the European and American powers represented at the Versailles Peace Conference remained noncommittal.

The Pan-African Congress reconvened in London in August 1921 and a month later in Brussels. Both meetings featured representatives from the Americas, the Caribbean, Europe, and Africa who echoed earlier Pan-Africanist reformist ideas, denouncing imperialism in Africa and racism in the United States. Moreover, the delegates demanded local self-government for colonial subjects and Du Bois stressed the need for increased interracial contacts between members of the black intelligentsia and those concerned about the political and economic status of colonial peoples.

In 1923, the Pan-African Congress met in two separate sessions in London and in Lisbon. Noted European intellectuals such as H. G. Wells and Harold Laski attended the London session. Several members of previous meetings participated in the deliberations that addressed the conditions of the African Diaspora as well as the global exploitation of black workers. While some scholars argue that the 1921 and 1923 congresses were effective only in keeping alive the idea of an oppressed people trying to abolish the yoke of discrimination, others claim that the international gatherings laid the foundation for the struggle that ultimately led to the political emancipation of the African continent.

Delegates reconvened for a fifth Pan-African Congress in New York in 1927. The congress featured 208 delegates from twenty-two American states and ten foreign countries. Africa, however, was represented only sparsely by delegates from the Gold Coast, Sierra Leone, Liberia, and Nigeria. The small number of African delegates was due in part to travel restrictions that the British and French colonial powers imposed on those interested in attending the congress, in an effort to inhibit further Pan-African gatherings. Most of the delegates were black Americans and many of them were women. The congress was primarily financed by Addie W. Hunton and the Women's International League for Peace and Freedom, an interracial organization that had been founded in 1919 by opponents of World War I. Similar to previous Pan- African congresses, participants discussed the status and conditions of black people throughout the world.

The financial crisis induced by the Great Depression and the military exigency generated by World War II necessitated the suspension of the Pan-African Congress for a period of eighteen years. In 1945, the organized movement was revived in Manchester, England. It is unclear whether Du Bois or George Padmore, a West Indian Marxist, provided the initiative for this meeting. Recognizing Du Bois's historic contribution to the Pan-African movement, delegates named him president of the 1945 congress. The Manchester meeting marked a turning point in the history of the gatherings. For the first time representatives of political parties from Africa and the West Indies attended the meetings. Moreover, the conservative credo of the forum gave way to radical social, political, and economic demands. Congress participants unequivocally demanded an end to colonialism in Africa and urged colonial subjects to use strikes and boycotts to end the continent's social, economic, and political exploitation by colonial powers.

While previous Pan-African congresses had been controlled largely by black middle-class British and American intellectuals who had emphasized the amelioration of colonial conditions, the Manchester meeting was dominated by delegates from Africa and Africans working or studying in Britain. The new leadership attracted the support of workers, trade unionists, and a growing radical sector of the African student population. With fewer African American participants, delegates consisted mainly of an emerging crop of African intellectual and political leaders, who soon won fame, notoriety, and power in their various colonized countries.

The final declaration of the 1945 congress urged colonial and subject peoples of the world to unite and assert their rights to reject those seeking to control their destinies. Congress participants encouraged colonized Africans to elect their own governments, arguing that the gain of political power for colonial and subject peoples was a necessary prerequisite for complete social, economic, and political emancipation. This politically assertive stance was supported by a new generation of African American activists such as the actor and singer Paul Robeson, the minister and politician Adam Clayton Powell, and the educator and political activist William A. Hunton Jr. who took an increasing interest in Africa.

While the Pan-African congresses lacked financial and political power, they helped to increase international awareness of racism and colonialism and laid the foundation for the political independence of African nations. African leaders such as Kwame Nkrumah of Ghana, Nnamdi Azikiwe of Nigeria, and Jomo Kenyatta of Kenya were among several attendees of congresses who subsequently led their countries to political independence. In May 1963, the influence of these men helped galvanize the formation of the Organization of African Unity (OAU), an association of independent African states and nationalist groups. Pan-Africanism is a movement initially inspired by Marcus Garvey (1887-1940) that seeks to unify African people living in Africa into a "One African Community" aimed at achieving economic, tribal, social and political unity. It advocated self-awareness on the part of Africans by encouraging the study of their history and culture. "Africa for Africans" was a slogan popularized by Marcus Garvey.

Pan- Africanism was put into effect in West Africa in Sierra Leone by Martin Delany (1812-1885), an African-American who developed his own re-emigration to Nigeria during 1859-1860. Edward Wilmot Blyden (1832-1912) adopted it when he arrived in West Africa in 1850. He was originally from St. Thomas and played a significant role in the emergence of Pan-Africanist ideas around the Atlantic through his public speeches and writings in Africa, Great Britain and the United States proposing the existence of an "African Personality" resembling contemporary European cultural nationalism. Blyden's idea's enforced the notion of race consciousness developed by W.E.B DuBois (1863-1963) at the end of the nineteenth century.

Pan-Africanism was the product of some extraordinary, European educated Africans and African-Americans who were most exposed to metropolitan culture and the influence of the modern world. Although the exact origins of Pan-Africanism are disputed the term first appeared in the 1890's from P.O Esedebe with the introduction of the Chicago Congress on Africa held in 1893. This marked the transition of Pan-Africanism from an idea to a movement and it is there that the word was first used. In their collection of Pan-African history, however, Adi and Sherwood highlight the creation of the African Association in 1898 and the convening of the first Pan-African Conference in 1900 in London both organised by the Trinidadian Lawyer Henry Sylvester Williams (1869-1911). The conference objective was of "bringing into closer touch with each other the peoples of African descent throughout the world."

W.E.B DuBois played an important role in developing the idea of Pan-Africanism and marshaling a transnational political movement around it. Indeed, DuBois contributed significant speeches to the proceedings of the Chicago Congress and the Pan-African 1900 Conference. DuBois soon initiated his own movement, which resulted in five Pan-African Congresses which were held in 1919 in Paris; 1921 in London, Brussels and Paris; in 1923 in London and Lisbon; in 1927 in New York; and in 1945 in Manchester England which was co-chaired by Kwame Nkrumah.

The main reason for the unification of Africa is purely socially and economically driven. A united gross domestic product (GDP) will enable Africa to form one currency which will enable the African currency to compete against the US dollar and the EURO in the world markets. The United Countries of Africa (UCA) has been in its infant stage for far too long in its current form as the Organisation of African Unity (OAU) now the African Union (AU). This is due to the post-colonial hangovers and influences from the former colonial rulers who still have a vast influence on the economic development of each country they once ruled. Even though all African countries have gained their independence from their imperialist colonial rulers, we are still heavily dependent upon their governmental systems; aid; educational; industrial and commercial trade links. Most countries are still being exploited for their natural resources through the funding of rebel movements by their former colonial rulers which in-turn causes a distraction within the country as they continue to plunder our natural minerals.

Africa has a rich natural cultural heritage of "UBUNTU" which is "African Cultural Togetherness and Unity". We as Africans need to socialise in order for growth in the arts and music. We must start setting targets to achieve Millennium Development Goals which will fulfil African Society aims and which can only be fulfilled through the unification and by the people of Africa working towards a common goal. The Abuja Treaty of June 1991 established The African Economic Community which also included African Leaders Declaration on HIV/AIDS and ORID.

Africa should unite for the sake of the next generation to grow up in a liberated society which will enable us to propose in all our endeavours and for the sake of our history. We Africans owe it our ancestors; ourselves; our children and their children to put in place a Social Service Structure which will enable us to assist and inspire the next generation to develop without any hindrance. We Africans have a rich history of togetherness (Ubuntu); of royal times; of our liberation leaders and their movements. We all need to read it to understand the past which will enable us to determine our future. This book is for every African black; white and Indian or whatever creed you are and for as long as you were born in Africa.

They have been several attempts by African Leaders to initiate unification such as The Arusha Declaration of 5th February 1967 which was initiated by Julius Nyerere; The Monrovia Symposium and Ababa Declaration of 1973; The Lagos Plan of Action was signed in 1980. The Final Act of Lagos of was signed by the African Union in 2000 and the Khartoum and Addis Ababa Declaration 15-16 January 2007.

The African Spirit GO CONFIDENTLY IN THE DIRECTION OF YOUR DREAMS, LIVE THE LIFE YOU HAVE IMAGINED...Thoreau. Wise book of Proverbs "Wine makes you mean, beer makes you quarrelsome a staggering drunk is not much fun. Quick-tempered leaders are like mad dogs cross them and they bite your head off. It's a mark of good character to avert quarrels, but fools love to pick fights. A farmer too lazy to plant in the spring has nothing to harvest in the fall.

Knowing what is right is like deep water in the heart; a wise person draws from the well within. Lots of people claim to be loyal and loving, but where on earth can you find one? God-loyal people, living honest lives, make it much easier for their children. Leaders who know their business and care keep a sharp eye out for the shoddy and cheap, For who among us can be trusted to be always diligent and honest? Switching price tags and padding the expense account are two things God hates.

Young people eventually reveal by their actions if their motives are on the up and up. Ears that hear and eyes that see we get our basic equipment from God ! Don't be too fond of sleep; you'll end up in the poorhouse. Wake up and get up; then there'll be food on the table. The shopper says, "That's junk I'll take it off your hands," then goes off boasting of the bargain. Drinking from the beautiful chalice of knowledge is better than adorning oneself with gold and rare gems. Hold tight to collateral on any loan to a stranger; beware of accepting what a transient has pawned. Stolen bread tastes sweet, but soon your mouth is full of gravel. Form your purpose by asking for counsel, then carry it out using all the help you can get. Gossips can't keep secrets, so never confide in blabbermouths. Anyone who curses their father and mother extinguishes light and exists benighted. A bonanza at the beginning is no guarantee of blessing at the end. Don't ever say, "I'll get you for that!" Wait for God; he'll settle the score.

God hates cheating in the marketplace; rigged scales are an outrage. The very steps we take come from God; otherwise how would we know where we're going? An impulsive vow is a trap; later you'll wish you could get out of it. After careful scrutiny, a wise leader makes a clean sweep of rebels and dolts. God is in charge of human life, watching and examining us inside and out. Love and truth form a good leader; sound leadership is founded on loving integrity. Youth may be admired for vigour, but grey hair gives prestige to old age. A good thrashing purges evil; punishment goes deep within us. (Proverbs 20:1-30 MSG)

It's easy to get distracted and demotivated by negative opinion, however if you really intend working towards achieving something worthwhile, you have to stay true to your beliefs and aspirations no matter how insignificant they may seem to other's. Long term strategies require a lot of patience and self-confidence, the best thing about them is you can always be proud of having made that effort to work towards achieving set objectives, it's always better to start and make mistakes along the way than to contemplate starting out of fear of being labelled a failure or associated with failure. "If you take responsibility and blame yourself, you have the power to change things. But if you put responsibility on someone else, then you are giving them the power to decide your fate."

The best feeling in the world is fianally knowing you took a step in the right direction. A step towards the future, like I have by writing this book now I feel great and inspired I am taking a step towards my future where everything is possible i.e I become a best seller l.o.l......As you start and end your day, be thankful for every little thing in your life. You will come to realize how blessed you truly are...by Killian F Bukutu ROMANS 8:18 FOR I CONSIDER THAT THE SUFFERINGS OF THIS PRESENT TIME ARE NOT WORTHY TO BE COMPARED WITH THE GLORY WHICH SHALL BE REVEALED IN US... LIFE IS AMAZING AND I AM GLAD THAT I WAS BORN TO LIVE MY LIFE AS I HAVE BEEN TRUELY BLESSED!!!!!!!!!.....THANKS YOU LORD FOR ALL YOUR GRACE AND ACKNOWLEDGEMENT I ONLY HAVE YOU TO THANK FOR ALL MY OPPORTUNITIES THAT YOU SEEM TO ALWAYS SHOWER ME WITH THANKS AGAIN....AMEN It's time for Africa to waken and embrace their own spirituality and Unite to become a formable force in world affairs.